A Book for All Believers

Simple Answers to Not So Simple Questions

TOM CASTOR

Always be ready to give an answer to anyone who asks you about the hope you have. Be ready to give the reason for it. But do it gently and with respect.

1 Peter 3:15

linguistically simple, theologically clear, biblically faithful

www.clearandsimplemedia.org

ISBN 978-1-7351640-7-6

Permission requests can be sent via the CONTACT page at www.clearandsimplemedia.org.

Scripture passages in this book are based on four Bible translations that are designed with an ESL reader in mind.

New International Readers Version (NIrV)
Copyright© 1995, 1998, 2014 by Biblica, Inc.

Easy-to-Read Version (ERV)
Copyright© 2006 by Bible League International

EasyEnglish Bible
Copyright© 2016 by MissionAssist (Wycliffe Associates) Worcestershire, UK

New Life Version
Copyright© 1969, 2003 Barbour Publishing, Inc.

Table Of Contents

Preface

For many years, God's people have used a collection of questions and answers to help them teach new believers. They use these questions and answers to teach the truths that are most important to them. This book will offer these important truths to a new group of people who follow Jesus.

This book contains 144 Questions and Answers. Each of the Questions and Answers are followed by a short set of words that explain the answers. These short chapters should help you better understand the answers.

This book is written with readers of English as a Second Language in mind. We wrote it in a way that makes translation into other languages simpler.

Each question is followed by an answer. Each answer is followed by selections from the Bible.* Each Bible selection includes the title of the book, (for example: Genesis). The book name is followed by the chapter where the selection is found (for example: chapter 2). This is followed by the verse or verses where the selection is found (for example: verse 3). So, Genesis chapter two and verse three would look like this: Genesis 2:3.

Foreword

When you read this book, it does not take long before you notice something. Jesus* is very important to the people who wrote it. There are many reasons for that. For example, many people say that Jesus was a prophet.* They say that Jesus spoke for God. We believe that too. But we believe that Jesus was much more than a prophet.

Other people say that Jesus was a wise man, a teacher. And during his life, Jesus taught many true and helpful things. We believe that too. But we believe that Jesus was much more than a wise teacher.

Some people say that Jesus was a good example to follow. He lived the kind of life that all people should try to live. We believe that too. If we all lived as Jesus did, we would be better people. The world would be a better place. But we believe that Jesus was much more than a good example.

So, What Do We Believe About Jesus?

At the end of this book is a short story to answer that question. If you are a new believer, that is a good place to start. Or perhaps you are not a follower* of Jesus at all. Then before you read the rest of the book, start with The Story of Jesus. That story begins on page 285 of this book. We hope that, if you have never heard the story, God will use those words to speak to you. And then, perhaps, you will come to love Jesus just as we do.

Introduction

Introduction

What kind of book is this?

Simple Answer to not so Simple Questions is a book of questions and answers. We wrote the book to help people understand what the Bible* teaches. Some people call a book like this a catechism. If the word catechism does not sound familiar to you, do not be too surprised. People do not use the word today as they did in the past. The word comes from a Greek* word that means to teach. You can find the word in the Bible in places like Luke 1:4, Acts 18:24-25, and Galatians 6:6.

How did we put the book together?

This little book uses the questions from our book called Simple Truths for the New Believer.* All of the questions and answers from that book are also in this one. But this book explains those questions and answers. When questions and answers cover some of the same ideas, we put them together. So some chapters in the book talk about more than one question and answer. The chapters in the book are short. The short answers help to make the book easy to read and remember. That makes the book a useful tool for teaching people the basic truths about our Lord* Jesus* Christ.*

Near the end of this book, you will find a Word List. Any word in this book with an * beside it is found in that list. Beside each word on the Word List is a definition of the word. The Word List will tell you what each of the words mean. Sometimes a word will have more than one meaning. This list will include the meanings that will help you understand what you read.

There are 144 questions and answers divided into 5 parts.

THE FIVE PARTS OF SIMPLE TRUTHS

PART ONE   **God** *and* **Man**
Questions 1 to 26

PART TWO   **Sin*** *and* **Law***
Questions 27 to 62

PART THREE   **Christ*** *and* **Salvation***
Questions 63 to 90

PART FOUR   **Spirit*** *and* **Church***
Questions 91 to 117

PART FIVE   **Prayer** *and* **Hope***
Questions 118 to 144

The Bible and 'Simple Answers'

Always remember, this book does not take the place of the Scriptures,* the Bible. It is a tool to help you understand the Word of God, not to draw you away from it. That is why you will see a list of Bible verses under each question and answer and at the bottom of many of the pages. These verses show where to find the answers in the Bible. There are many more verses we could have included with each answer. But these are included to help you get a good start.

PART 1

God *and* Man

QUESTIONS 1 TO 26

question ——
001

Who made you?

God made me.

Genesis 1:26-27 • Genesis 2:7 • Acts 17:26

question ——
002

What else did God make?

God made all things.

Genesis 1:31 • Psalm 33:6-9 • Colossians 1:16-17

God made all things. He tells us this in the first words of the Bible.* He made the things that we can see. He made mountains and trees. He made animals and birds. He made the clouds and the stars. And God made the things that we cannot see. He made the air that we breathe. He made the angels.* He made all of these things. He made all things and he owns all things. The Bible tells us that God is Lord.* There is no one greater than God. There is no one that has more power than God.

God made all things, but no one made God. He is not a part of creation.* He is the Creator.* He is the Maker of heaven* and earth. He does not need the things he made so he can live. He made all things because it pleased him to do so. But he does not need anything.

The last thing that God made was a man and a woman. He made a man named Adam.* He made a woman named Eve.* He made them in a different way than he made all other things. He made man from the dust of the ground. He made woman from a bone from the side of the man. He also made them to be different from anything else that he made. The scripture* says that he made them 'in his own image.' Adam and Eve were the special creation of God. They were like God in a way that no other thing that God made, was like him.

When God made all things, he made some things that could grow and make new things just like themselves. He made plants to grow fruit and make seeds. Those seeds could then make new plants to grow. God made the man and the woman like this too. The man and the woman could come together and make children. They could make sons and daughters. The Bible says that every son and daughter they made was just like them. Their children and their children's children were all made 'in the image of God.'

We are made in the image of God

So, we are made in the image of God too. God made us in a different way than he made our first parents. But he made us just as much as he made them. He makes every person that is born. He makes them all 'in the image of God.'

One of the Psalms tells us that God watches over everyone that is born. Before we are born, God puts us together. He was there with us when we were inside our mother's body.

'You created* the deepest parts of my being.
    You put me together inside my mother's body.
How you made me is amazing and wonderful.
    I praise* you for that.
What you have done is wonderful.
    I know that very well.
None of my bones was hidden from you
    when you made me inside my mother's body.
    That place was as dark as the deepest parts of
    the earth.
When you were putting me together there,
    your eyes saw my body even before it was
    formed.'[1]

God made Adam and Eve. God made you. God made everyone else too. And he makes all people in his own image.

---

1. Psalm 139:13-16

Why did God make you and all things?

God made me and all things for his own glory.*

Psalm 19:1 • Isaiah 43:7 • 1 Corinthians 10:31

The word 'glory' is an important word in the Bible.* You will find the word in many places. You will also find that the Bible uses the word in more than one way.

When God led Moses* and the people out of Egypt,* they did not have enough food. God decided that he would provide food for the people. But first, he showed them that he was present among them. He appeared to the people in a bright cloud. The light that surrounded God when he appeared is called the glory of God.

Later, this bright cloud led the people through the desert. It was like a cloud of fire. When Moses went up on the mountain to talk to God, this cloud covered the mountain.[1] Many years later, this cloud surrounded God's tent in the camp where God's people lived. Then, this bright cloud came into the temple* that Solomon* built. When the cloud entered the temple, this was a sign that God had come to live among the people. When the people saw this, they described it as the glory of God.

In the New Testament,* we read about the glory of God in this way as well. When Jesus came, he was God living among them. One day, Jesus took some of his friends up on a mountain. Moses and Elijah* appeared to them. And Jesus' clothes began to shine like a bright light. God had shown himself to his people in the past in this way. Now, these men saw this glory in the person of Jesus.

Some day, God will make a new heaven* and a new earth. This new heaven and new earth will need no sun. The light of the glory of God will be the only light that will be needed there.

The word glory can also describe the great things that are true about God. In English, we can use the word 'see' to mean 'understand.' Sometimes, when someone says, 'I see,' they are saying 'Now I know. Now I understand.' So, when we come to know how excellent God is, we can say that we see his glory.

The writers of the New Testament use the word glory in this way most often. They 'saw' the glory of God in Jesus. They did not see Jesus in a bright cloud in the way Moses saw God. Jesus was God in human form. They saw God's glory in the way Jesus lived among them. They understood God's glory in what Jesus said to them. They saw God's glory in the way he died. They saw God's glory in Jesus when God raised him up from the dead. They saw God's glory when he went up to heaven to be with the Father again. They came to understand who God was in a new way when they saw him in Jesus.[2] When they saw Jesus, they could see in him God's goodness and beauty and wisdom. They saw that God was just and merciful* when they saw those qualities in Jesus.

Some day, Jesus will return to the earth. He will sit to judge all people. Jesus will punish evil.* He will bless* his people. In those days, 'the whole earth will be filled with God's glory.'[3] Everyone on earth will see God for who he truly is. Everyone will see his glory.

The word glory can also mean value or honor.* So the Bible tells the people who follow God that they should 'give God glory.' That means that they are to show God the respect* and give him the praise* that he deserves.

'God made all things for his own glory.'[4] That is, God made all things as a way to show himself to us. When we see God in what he has made, we will give him the honor that he deserves.

David* says:

'The heavens tell about the glory of God.
The skies show that his hands made them.'[5]

God made all things. And all of the things that he made help people see him for all that he is. When people truly see God in the things he has made, this brings him glory.

---

1. Exodus 24:16-17; Exodus 40:34-35   3. Habakkuk 2:14   5. Psalm 19:1
2. 2 Corinthians 4:5-6   4. Psalm 19:1-4; Isaiah 43:6-7

question ——

004

How can you give glory* to God?

I give glory* to God when I love him and trust* him. And when I do what he tells me to do.

Matthew 5:16 • John 14:21 • 1 John 5:3

question ——

005

Why should you give glory to God?

Because he made me and takes care of me.

Psalm 145:9 • 1 Peter 5:7 • Revelation 4:11

God made us. After he made us, he did not leave us alone. God still watches over us. He takes care of us. He does not forget us. He knows all of the things that we think and all of the things that we do. God is always with us. God is always working for our good. God is always working in ways to complete his good purposes for us. That is why we should live in a way that gives glory to God.

The word glory sometimes means value or honor.* The Bible* tells the people who follow God that they should 'give God glory.' That means that they are to show God the respect and give him the praise* that he deserves. We can give glory to God in many ways. We can praise God by speaking well of him and singing praise to him. But we can and must also honor God in the things that we do.

01 **We give glory to God when we trust him.** All people have people in their lives that they trust. All people have people in their lives that they do not trust. When we trust someone, we show that we value their words to us. We believe that they will keep their promises. We believe that they have our best interests in mind. When we trust God in this way, we honor him.

02 **We give glory to God when we love him.** God wants us to love him with all of our heart,* all of our mind, and all of our strength. Everyone has people in their lives that they love. But God wants us to love him more than we love anyone or anything else. When we do, it brings glory to God.[1]

03 **We give glory to God when we obey him.** Jesus said that the person who truly loves God obeys his commands. When we do what God tells us to do, we show that we want to please him. We show that we respect his authority over us. We show that we believe that he knows what is best for us.[2] This brings him glory.

We are to trust God fully. We are to love God with all of our heart, all of our mind, and all of our strength. We are to listen to him and obey his words. When we do, we give glory to God.

And, when we trust, love, and obey God, we can cause other people to give glory to God as well. When we watch children who are kind and show respect to others, we think well of their parents. In the same way, when people see our good works, it will cause them to 'give glory to our Father in heaven.'*³

GOD IS ALWAYS WORKING FOR OUR GOOD.

Because God is good, we honor him when we do what is good. Because God is love, we honor him when we show love for other people. Because God is wise, we honor him when we make wise choices. Because God forgives,* we honor him when we forgive other people. Because God has been generous to us, we honor him when we are generous to the weak and those in need. When people see us live good lives in these ways, they give glory to the God we serve.

---

1. Philippians 1:9-11
2. Matthew 5:16; 1 Corinthians 10:31
3. 1 Peter 2:11-12

question —— 006

How many gods are there?

There is only one God.

Deuteronomy 6:4 • Isaiah 45:5 • Jeremiah 10:10

question —— 007

In how many persons does this one God exist?

God exists in three persons.

Matthew 3:16-17 • John 5:23 • John 10:30 • John 15:26

question —— 008

Who are they?

The Father, the Son, and the Holy Spirit.*

Matthew 28:19 • 2 Corinthians 13:14 • 1 Peter 1:2

All Christians believe in the Trinity.*

'There is only one God.
This God exists in three persons.'

All Christians believe this. They believe it because that is what the scriptures* teach. When they want to talk about this idea, they use a special word. That word is trinity.

This word is never found in the Bible.* But it helps to teach an important truth about God. The word is made from putting two other words together. Those words are 'three' and 'unity.' So, trinity means 'three in unity' or 'three in one.'

What are people saying when they use this word?

There is one God. And this one God exists in three persons.

We cannot explain how this can be. But this is what the scriptures say about God.

01 There is only one God.[1]

02 We read about a person called Father. He is called God. We read about a person called the Son. He is also called God. We read about the Spirit.* He is also called God.[2]

We are told that all three persons are the one true God. All three persons can do what only God can do. They are all to be given honor* that belongs to the one, true God. When believers* are told to praise* God, they are told to honor all three persons as one God.

When we put those things together, this is what we can say. There is only one God. But this God exists in three persons: God the Father, God the Son, and God the Holy Spirit.

We may also say it this way. The Father is the same God as the Son and the Holy Spirit. But the Father is not the same person as the Son or the Holy Spirit. The same is true for the Son and the Spirit. They are all the same God. But they are not the same person.

God has always been one God in three persons. God will always be one God in three persons. Each of these persons is equal with the other. They are equal in power, wisdom, glory,* and honor. They are always in perfect agreement. They share the same love for each other. They are completely one.

God did not become Trinity only when Jesus came. God did not become this way only to do a special task. God does not merely seem to be this way. This is who God is.

This is very difficult to explain. God is like no one else. He is far above us and beyond us. He knows and understands all things. What we know is limited. We cannot understand his ways. We can see what the scriptures say about him. We can use those scriptures to describe him. But we cannot completely understand how these things can be so.

Sometimes, people use examples to help us understand.

Some say that God is like an egg. One egg is made of three parts. The shell is the egg. The white part inside is the egg. The yellow part inside is the egg. It takes all three parts to make one egg. But God is not divided into parts. God is not like an egg.

Some say that God is like water. Water is always water. It can be ice when it gets very cold. Sometimes, it can become steam when it is very hot. Most of the time, it is a liquid. But water cannot be ice, steam, and liquid at the same time. God is not like water.

Some say that God is like a person. One man can be a son, a father, and a brother at the same time. One man is three different men in that sense. But a man cannot be a father and a son and a brother to the same person. God is not like a man.

These pictures can sometimes be helpful. They do explain how something can be three things and also be one. But they are not three in one in the same way that God is. We have no perfect example of anything else that is just like God is.

So, we can say that this is what the scriptures teach us about God. We can describe what it teaches by using the word trinity. We cannot completely understand how God can be as he is. But, when we look at the scriptures,* we cannot deny that this is what it says.

The Father is God.
The Son is God.
The Holy Spirit is God.

The Father is not the Son or the Holy Spirit. The Son is not the Holy Spirit or the Father. The Holy Spirit is not the Father or the Son. But all three persons are fully God.

There is one God. This one God forever exists in three persons.

---

1. Deuteronomy 6:4-5; Isaiah 45:5-6; 1 Corinthians 8:5-6

2. Philippians 1:2; Hebrews 1:8; Acts 5:3-4

What is God?

God is spirit.* He does not have a body like men.

John 4: 24 • 2 Corinthians 3:17 • 1 Timothy 1:17

'God is Spirit. Those who worship* him must worship him in spirit and in truth.'[1]

God is spirit. God does not have a body like we do. A house can be made of wood or stones. We are made of skin and bones. But God is not made of skin or bones. God is not made of parts or pieces like the things that he created.* He is spirit. He is different from any of the things that he made. He is not made of anything that we find in creation.*

Because he is spirit, the things that limit us cannot limit God. Because we have a body, we grow old. We grow tired. Our minds grow weak. God does not have a body. So, he does not grow old or tired. Because God is spirit, he has no shape or size. He cannot be measured like the things that he made. We cannot weigh him. We cannot find where he begins or ends. He cannot be limited to one place or one time. No place can hold God inside it. Because he is spirit, he can be in all places at one time. He is always present. He is present in all places. He is present at all times.

Although God is spirit and does not have a body, he is a true person. God cares for people. He thinks and acts and decides. God speaks to people. And God listens to his people. He hears and answers people when they pray. He is alive in every way. In fact, the scriptures* say that he is life. It is God who gives life to all things that live.[2] All life comes from God because he is life.

There are places where the scriptures speak about God as if he does have a body. They may speak of God's eyes or hands or arm. For example, 'God rules by his power forever. His eyes watch the nations.'[3] But, when the Bible* speaks this way, it does not mean that God has eyes like we do. The scriptures use those words to tell us that God can see. He can see us. He can see all things. When the Bible says that God has hands, it does not mean that

God has hands like our hands. Those words tell us that God can act. God can make things. He can do things like a person might do with their hands. When the Bible says that God has an arm, it means to tell us that God is strong.[4] He is great and has great power. He can overcome anyone who stands against him. He can protect his people from their enemies. He can remove anything that stands in his way.

God can overcome anyone who stands against him.

1. John 4:24
2. Acts 17:25
3. Psalm 66:7
4. Psalm 89:13

Did God have a beginning?

No, God has always been and God will always be.

Exodus 3:14 • Psalm 90:2 • Isaiah 40:28

Does God change?

No, God is always the same.

Psalm 102:26-27 • Malachi 3:6 • Hebrews 13:8

Everything we can see had a beginning. All people had a beginning. The heavens and the earth had a beginning. They began when God made them.[1] Even the things that we cannot see had a beginning. The angels* are spirits* that serve and worship* God. We do not know when God made them, but they were present when he made the earth.[2] But long before there was anything else, there was God. He made all things. Nothing was made that he did not make. But no one made God. He had no beginning. He will have no end. He always was. He is now. He will always be.[3]

So, God has always been and God is perfect. He needed nothing else to make him complete. God did not need to learn. He has always known all things. He did not need to grow stronger. He has always had all power. He has perfect control of all things. Because he was perfect from the beginning, he has never needed to change.

Everything we know about changes. People change. The earth changes. We change. When a thing changes, it can change in many ways. It can change to become better. It can change to become worse. It can change to become something different than it was. But God is perfect.[4] He cannot change to become better than he is, because he is already perfect. Because he is perfect, he would not change to be less than he is. God will never be anything other than the perfect God. This is why the scriptures* tell us that God does not change.

God never changes. But it is also true that God is a God who shows mercy* to people. There are stories in the Bible* that show this. God would send a prophet* with a message. The prophet would tell the people that God was about to judge them because of the evil* things that they were doing. But the people listened to the prophet's words. They turned away from the evil things they were doing. So, God did not judge the people. His judgement* changed to mercy. But God did not change when he chose not to judge them. He has always been a 'loving God who shows mercy.'[5] This is who God is. He can show mercy to anyone he wishes to show mercy to.[6] This is the way that God truly is. That is the way he has always been. He delights to show mercy to people who turn away from evil and turn to him.

Think about it this way. A man is riding his bicycle to town. He is riding into a strong wind. The wind makes it very hard for him to go down the road. We could say that the wind is against him. Then he turns to go home. He begins to go back the way he came. Now the wind is not against him. Instead, the wind is helping him. If we told someone about his ride, we might say this. 'The wind changed. It was against him. But on his way back home, it helped him.' That is one way we could tell the story. And everyone would understand what we were saying. But the wind did not change. The man changed.

We call him the EVERLASTING GOD.

And the everlasting God does not change.

The scriptures tell us that when a person or a nation is doing evil, God is against them. He will judge them for the evil that they are doing. But when a person or a nation turns from their evil way, God may choose not to judge them. He may show them mercy instead. That is the kind of God that he is.

God had no beginning. He will have no end. This is what we mean when we call him the everlasting* God. And the everlasting God does not change.

---

1. Psalm 102:25
2. Job 38:4-7
3. Revelation 1:8

4. Psalm 18:30
5. Jonah 4:1-2; Joel 2:13-14
6. Exodus 33:19

question —— 012

Where is God?

God is everywhere

Psalm 139:7-12 • Jeremiah 23:23-24 • Acts 17:27-28

question —— 013

Can you see God?

No, I cannot see God, but he always sees me.

Psalm 33: 13-15 • Proverbs 5:21 • John 1:18
1 Timothy 1:17

We cannot see God. The scriptures* say this many times and in many places.[1] But there are places in the scriptures that say that a person or a group of people did see God.[2] How can both of these be true?

Because God is spirit,* we cannot see God on our own. But God is not hidden from us. He is a God who has shown himself to us. He wants us to know him.

The scriptures say that we can see God by looking at the things that he has done. We cannot see the wind, but we see what the wind does. It moves the branches of the trees. It blows the dust on the road. We can see that God is there in the same way, even when we cannot see him.

We can also see God through the things that he has made. We can see God because he is at work in the world. He provides food for the animals.[3] He sends the rain.[4] He gives the harvest.[5]

We can also see God in the stories from the scriptures. We see God as he acted to help his people. He chose Abraham.* He promised that Abraham's family would bless* the world. He guided Abraham. He gave him a son. Then he rescued his people out of Egypt.* He guided them through the desert. He gave them his law.* He gave them the land that he had promised to them.

Sometimes, God did appear to his people so that they could see him. God appeared to Adam* and Eve.* They spoke with God. They heard him, and he listened to them. We do not know what they saw of God. But we do know that they knew him. They knew that he was present with them. He appeared to Abraham as a man. He appeared to Jacob* as an angel.* And he came to Israel* as a cloud of fire. Then, when God wanted to show himself to us, he came to live among us. He sent his Son, Jesus. He became a man and lived among us. Jesus came to make God known.

But no man has ever seen all of God as he is in all of his glory.* So we cannot see God because he cannot be seen. But God always sees us. He always sees us because he is everywhere we are. In fact, God is everywhere. All of God is present, in all places, all of the time. There is no place that God is not. God can always see us because God is everywhere.

The scriptures tell us this in many places and in many ways. Look at this song that King David* wrote:

> 'Where can I go from Your Spirit?
>> Or where can I run away from where you are?
> If I go up to heaven,* you are there!
>> If I make my bed in the place of the dead, you
>> are there!
> If I take the wings of the morning or live far away
>> on the sea,
> Even there your hand will lead me,
>> And Your right hand will hold me.'[6]

David knows that he can never escape from God. God always sees us. He is always present with us. So David gives thanks to God.

God is always there, in all places, at all times. This is not such good news for those who do bad things. The wicked cannot hide what they do from God. God sees them. God is there, even when they think that he cannot find them.

But this is good news for God's people. Because he is always present, we can know that he will not forget us. We know that he is always able to hear us. We can speak to God wherever we are. We do not need to travel to a special place to find him.

Sometimes, in scripture, it may seem that God is only in one place at one time. God can do special things to make his people know that he is near to them. The scriptures tell us that God can be present in special ways in special places. The scriptures even speak of God coming to a place or going from a place. These are special ways that God can make people know that he is near. But the scriptures always remind us that God is always present, in all places, at all times.

'God is our place of safety. He is always there to help us in times of trouble.' He is never far away from us. He is always able to rescue us. We are never alone.

---

1. Romans 1:20; Colossians 1:15; Hebrews 11:27
2. Genesis 16:13; Genesis 32:30; Exodus 24:1; Isaiah 9:1
3. Matthew 6:26; Psalm 147:9
4. Job 5:10; Psalm 147:8
5. Psalm 65:9-13; Psalm 104:14,15
6. Psalm 139:7-12

question —— 014

Does God know all things?

Yes, God knows all things. I cannot hide anything from God.

1 Samuel 2:3 • Proverbs 15:3 • Hebrews 4:13

question —— 015

Can God do all things?

Yes, God can do every holy* thing that he desires.

Isaiah 46:9-10 • Daniel 4:34-35 • Ephesians 1:11

The scriptures* tell us in many places that God is in control.[1] If God is in control of all things, two things must be true. God must know all things. And God must have power that has no limit. The scriptures tell us that he has both.

01 God knows all things.

God knows everything.[2] There is not one thing that God does not know. He knows all that has happened in the past. He knows all things that are happening now. He knows all things that will happen in the future.[3] He knows all things, great and small. He knows what is happening in the heart* of the king. He knows when a small bird falls to the ground. He knows the number of hairs on your head.[4]

God also knows about each person in a personal way. God saw us before we were born. He knew us when we were still growing in our mother's body. God knows everything about us. He knows every thought that we are thinking. He knows what our hearts and minds imagine. He even knows the things that we have done wrong that we thought were secret.[5]

The scriptures say it this way:
'You know when I sit down and when I get up.
    You know my thoughts from far away.
You know where I go and where I lie down.
    You know everything I do.
Lord,* you know what I want to say,
    even before the words leave my mouth.'
    (Psalm 139:2-4)

Because God knows all things, he is a perfect judge. A judge must listen to what people say. He must decide who is telling the truth. He must try to understand why a person did something. And he must make a wise choice to reward them or to punish them. God knows all things. He knows our thoughts. He knows why we do the things that we do. He knows the whole truth. So he will be wise when he judges.[6]

02 God has all power.

Sometimes, the scriptures speak about what God knows and what God can do in the same verse.[7]

'It is God who made the earth by his power. He made the world by his wisdom. By his understanding, he has spread out the heavens.'[8]

God 'built the earth by his wisdom.' So, when he made all things, he knew how he wanted the world to become. When he saw what he had made, it was good. It was just as he had planned it to be. He made it all from nothing.[9] He needed no tools. He needed no help. He spoke, and it was so. He made the seas. He made the stars. He made the mountains. He made all things with the power of a word,[10] by the breath of his mouth.[11] And God did not leave the world alone after he made it. He now holds the world together.[12] He causes it to continue. One day follows the next. He keeps the seas in their places. He gives rain to the earth. He makes food grow to feed the animals.

It is God who made the earth by his power.

God does as he pleases.[13] No enemy can defeat the God of heaven.*[14] No one can keep him from doing what he has decided to do. The nations and their armies are nothing to him. They are like a drop of water in a bucket. They are like dust. And nothing is too hard for God.[15] He can make the world with his words. He can make the sun stand still in the sky. He can give a son to a woman who could not have children. He can raise a man and make him alive after he had died. There is nothing too hard for God.

But there are some things that God cannot do. He cannot lie. He cannot sin.* He cannot make a promise and then fail to do what he promised. God cannot do these things. But it is not because God is weak. He cannot do these things because he is good. God is holy. All that he does is holy and just, pure and true. There is no weakness in God. He can do every holy thing that he wants to do.

1. Isaiah 14:26; Isaiah 46:10
2. 1 John 3:20
3. Isaiah 46:9-10
4. Proverbs 21:1; Matthew 10:29-30
5. Psalm 90:9; Ezekiel 8:12

6. Jeremiah 17:10; 1 Samuel 2:3
7. Psalm 147:5
8. Jeremiah 10:12
9. Hebrews 11:3
10. Hebrews 1:3

11. Psalm 33:6
12. Colossians 1:3
13. Job 23:13; Psalm 115:3
14. Psalm 24:7-8
15. Genesis 18:14; Luke 1:37

question 016

Where do I learn how to know, to trust,* to love and to obey God?

God has shown me how to know, to trust, to love and to obey him in his word, the Bible.*

Psalm 119:104-105 • John 20:30-31 • 2 Timothy 3:15

question 017

What does the Bible teach you?

The Bible teaches me the truth about God and his plan to rescue the world through Jesus* Christ.* And it teaches me the truth about myself.

Psalm 119:159-160 • John 17:17 • 2 Timothy 3:14-17

question 018

Who wrote the Bible?

Men who were guided and taught by the Holy Spirit.*

2 Peter 1:20-21 • 2 Peter 3:15-16

The Bible is like other books in many ways. But there is one way that the Bible is like no other book. In fact, it is the only book of its kind. The Bible is the word of God.

What does it mean to say that the Bible is God's word? We mean that the Bible is a revelation* from God. We are saying that the words of the Bible come to us as a message from God himself.

God has many ways to show us things about himself. For example, God made all things. When he did, he left many signs in his creation* that tell us things about him. When we look at what he made, we can see that he has great power. We can know that he must be very wise. We can see that God likes order and beauty. We can know these things about God by looking at all that he has made.

But there are many things that we cannot know about God just by looking about us. That is why God gave us the Bible. God tells us things in the Bible that we could not know without it. The Bible tells who God is. It tells us why God made us. It tells us what is wrong with the world. It tells us how God will make everything better some day. We could not know these things unless God chose to tell us. And God has chosen to tell us in the Bible. If God had not given us the Bible, we would know almost nothing about him. And we would know almost nothing about his son, Jesus.

The Bible is the word of God. How does the Bible tell us these things? The Bible uses words. It is a book with words and sentences just like other books. But there is one very important difference. The words that are in the Bible come to us from God. That is why we sometimes call the Bible the scripture.* They are God's words in writing. So, when we read the Bible, we are reading God's words. When we listen to the words from the Bible, we are hearing from God. The Bible is not just some men's ideas and thoughts about God. They are the thoughts and words of God himself.

So men wrote the words in the Bible and the words are the words of God. But how can that be? How can human words be God's words too? The Bible tells us. Sometimes, God told men just what to say. But, sometimes, men wrote just what they wanted to say. And, as they wrote, God helped them. The Bible does not tell us just how God did this. The Bible only tells us that these men were 'carried along' by God's Spirit.*[1] The writers did not just write the words as they heard them from God. Nor did God just give them ideas about what to write. The Bible says that the written words are 'God breathed.'[2] What the human writers wrote is what God wanted to say to us. The words that they wrote tell us what God wanted us to know.

We should read the Bible because there is no other book like it. The Bible comes to us from God.

---

1. 2 Peter 1:21   2. 2 Peter 3:16

Who were our first parents?

Adam* and Eve.*

Genesis 3:20 • Genesis 5:1-2

How did God make our first parents?

God made the body of Adam out of the dust from the ground. God made Eve from the body of Adam.

Genesis 2:7 • Genesis 2:21-23 • Genesis 3:19
Psalm 103:14

In the beginning was God. And God created* everything. He spoke. And when he did, he made the whole world and everything in it. God said, 'Let there be light' And there was – light. Then God made the skies, and the land and the water. And he made all the trees and plants that cover the earth. He made the sun, and the moon and the stars. He filled the seas with fish. He filled the sky with birds. He made all the animals that walk on the earth. And God saw all this and saw that it was good.

Then, God took some of the soil he had made and he formed a man. And he breathed into the man, and he began to live.

God took this man and put him in a garden that God had made for him. There were all kinds of trees there. And God put two trees in the middle of the garden. The fruit from one tree gave life. The other tree gave the knowledge of good and evil.* And God told the man,

> 'You can eat fruit from any tree in this garden. But you must not eat from the tree of the knowledge of good and evil. For if you eat from that tree, you will die.'

Now the man was alone. So God said,

> 'It is not good for man to be alone. I will make a companion for him.'

Then God put the man to sleep. He took a bone from the man's side. And from it, God made a woman.

And God put them both in the garden he made for them. He blessed* them. He told them to have many children and to fill the earth with people. And he told them to rule over the birds and the fish and all of the animals he had made.

The man was named Adam. The woman was named Eve. And they were both naked and felt no shame. Then God looked over all that he had made and saw that it was very good.[1]

This is the first part of the Bible* story. It is found in Genesis chapter one and two. Genesis chapter one tells us that God is the one who created all things. Genesis chapter two tells us the special story about how God made the first people. All other people came from Adam and Eve. That is why we call them our first parents.

When God made everything, the last thing he created was a man and a woman. And when God made them, he made them in a different way than he made everything else. When he made the sky and the seas and the land, he spoke. When God made Adam, he 'formed' him. God took some of the soil he had made, and shaped Adam from it. Then he breathed into Adam and Adam began to live.

God also made Eve in a different way than he made anything else. God took a bone from Adam's side and made her. God gave special time and care to make Adam and Eve. He did this because God would give them a special place in all of his creation.* He gave them a special place to live. He gave them a special job to do. And he made them to know him. They could know God in a way that no other thing that he made could know him.

The first chapters of the Bible show us that God blessed the man and the woman in a special way. God made a world for them to live in. He made the sun to give light so they could see. He made the air for them to breathe. He made water for them to drink. He gave them plants so they could eat. He made the world a special place where they could be with him. They could walk and talk with God there. He also gave them a job to do. He made the world in such a way that the world needed to be cared for. Adam and Eve were to help God take care of the world that he made.

All of the things that God made were good. And when God finished making Adam and Eve, he looked at all he had done. He could see that it was very good.

---

1. Genesis 1

021

How were Adam* and Eve* different from everything else that God had made?

God made Adam and Eve in his own image.

Genesis 1:26-27

022

How can we see God's image in Adam and Eve?

God gave them rule over his creation.* They could understand what is true. They could love what is right. They could enjoy what is beautiful. They could do what pleases God. They could talk with God and each other.

Genesis 1:26-27 • Genesis 2:7-9 • Psalm 147:10-11
Philippians 4:8

God made all things. But he did not make all things in the same way. God made the animals 'after their kind.' But, when he made a man and a woman, God made them in his own image.[1] The image of God was what set them apart from all other created* things.

What does it mean that man and woman are made in God's image?

Sometimes when we stand in the sun, we can see our shadow. The shadow is not you. But it is shaped like you in many ways. You can see that your shadow is different than someone else's shadow. In one sense, you see your image in the shadow. Or when we look into a clear pool of water, sometimes we see ourselves. The water reflects our image. When God made Adam and Eve, he made them to reflect who he is in certain ways.

God made the man and woman holy.* The word holy means 'set apart.' When we say, God is holy, we mean that he is set apart from his creation. God is one of a kind. He is the only true God. And he is set apart from evil.* He is good, so he is set apart from all that is not good. When we say that the man and the woman were holy, we mean that God set them apart from all of the other things that he made. They alone were made in the image of God. And they were good. God was pleased with them.

God does not have a body. But he gave the man and the woman a body to help them reflect his image. With this body, Adam and Eve could experience the world that God made. They could see. They could touch. They could smell the plants and trees in the garden. They could hear. They could taste the food that the garden provided for them.

God also gave them a purpose. And a body helped the man and the woman do the tasks that God gave them to do. God did not need a body to make a garden for them. But he gave a body to Adam and Eve so they could join God in caring for the garden.

God said,

> 'Have children so that there will be many of you.
> Fill the earth and bring it under your control. Rule
> over the fish in the seas and the birds in the sky.
> Rule over every living animal that moves along
> the ground.'[2]

God gave the man the job of giving names to all of the animals as well. As they did these things, they were to reflect God's image as the ruler over all that he made.

God gave Adam and Eve a mind to think as well. They knew many things from the moment God made them. They knew God. They knew each other. They knew themselves. But God also made them so that they could learn new things. They could listen to God and understand what he wanted them to do.

With their minds, the man and the woman could also imagine and create. They could not make things from nothing. Only God could do that. But they could imagine things that did not yet exist. And they could make those things with the hands that God gave them. They could create music. They could make art. They could use words to write a poem.

God made the man and the woman so they could speak. None of the animals could speak to God the way the man and the woman could. Adam and Eve could talk with God. And they could speak to one another. They could describe the world about them with words. They could say the things that they were thinking. God is a God who speaks. So, the man and the woman, made in his image, were able to speak as well.

There is one God. This God exists in three persons. The Trinity: God the Father, the Son, and the Holy Spirit, made all things. But before God made anything, the Father, Son, and Holy Spirit loved and honored one another. And when God made the man and the woman in his own image, he made them to know and to love God. He also made the man and the woman to know and love each other. As people made in God's image, they both could love and worship* God. And they could show love and honor to one another as well.

God made both the man and the woman in his image.[3] They enjoyed God and one another in the good place that he had made for them.

---

1. Genesis 5:1; Genesis 9:6;
  1 Corinthians 11:7; James 3:9

2. Genesis 1:26-28
3. Genesis 1:27

question —— 023

What did God give Adam* and Eve* other than bodies?

God gave them souls* that will never die.

Genesis 2:7 • Deuteronomy 6:5 • Ecclesiastes 12:7
Matthew 16:26

question —— 024

Do you have a soul as well as a body?

Yes, I have a soul that will never die.

Zechariah 12:1 • Acts 7:59 • 2 Corinthians 5:8

God made Adam and Eve in his own image. He gave them a body and a soul. The soul is sometimes called the spirit.*

When God created* Adam, God breathed life into him. Adam had a body. But God also gave Adam a soul.[1] This is one thing that makes a human being different than any other living thing that God made. God made nothing else in creation* this way.

All people have a body and a soul. God made both the soul and the body, so both the body and the soul are good. The body and the soul each had a beginning. They are not eternal* like God is. They only live as long as God decides to give them life. A body may die. But the scriptures* tell us that God will cause the soul to live somewhere forever.

When the body dies, the soul leaves the body. A body can die and be buried. But the soul continues to live. The soul continues as it was before the body died.

One story in the scriptures speaks of the soul after death.[2] Two men died. But, after they died, the souls of both men were still alive. Both men had gone to a place that was different than where they had been with their bodies. Both men knew who they were. They knew other people about them. They remembered what they had done in the past. Their souls continued after their bodies had died.

But all souls do not go to the same place. The scripture also tells us that the souls of those who love God go to be with Jesus.*[3] Those who did not love God while their souls were with their bodies are kept in another place. They wait there until the day God brings them to be judged.

Both our bodies and our souls are important to God. Some day, God will bring the souls of all people to return to their bodies again. All people will be raised from the dead.[4] Then they will be alive again, body and soul, to stand before God.

———

GOD MADE BOTH THE SOUL AND THE BODY, SO BOTH THE BODY AND THE SOUL ARE GOOD.

———

1. Ecclesiastes 12:7
2. Luke 16:19-31

3. Philippians 1:23;
2 Corinthians 5:8

4. Revelation 20:13

question —— **025**

What were Adam* and Eve* like when God made them?

God made them holy* and happy. They lived with God in the garden he made for them.

Genesis 1:26-28 • Genesis 2:15-17 • Genesis 2:25
Psalm 8:4-8

question —— **026**

What did God require of Adam and Eve?

God required them to trust* him and obey him completely.

Genesis 2:15-17 • Psalm 8:4-8

From the first day when God made him, Adam lived with God his maker. And the God who made him is holy.

What does it mean to be holy? The scriptures* tell us that God is holy. He is 'set apart.' He is set apart from all the things that he made. Because he is the one who made all things, he is greater than all that he made. He is higher than his creation* and nothing can compare with him. God is also 'set apart' from evil.* God is not only great, he is good. He always does what is right. God never does what is wrong. There is no evil mixed with his goodness. He is completely good.

God made Adam to be holy as well. Adam was not holy in the same way that God is holy. But Adam was also 'set apart' from all the other things that God made. God made him in his own image. Adam could speak, feel, think, imagine, and decide in ways that none of the animals could. Adam was also 'set apart' from evil. Adam walked and talked with God. He had no fear. He felt no shame or guilt.* He only felt God's pleasure. Being with God gave him joy.[1]

Adam was 'set apart' from all the other things that God made.

God gave Adam a place of honor.* He asked Adam to name all the animals. He gave Adam and Eve the task to work and keep the garden. He told them to have many children. He told Adam to rule over all that God had made. And Adam showed honor to God. Adam trusted him. He had a desire to please God. He always did as God asked.

God also gave Adam many other reasons to be happy. God made a wonderful place for him to live. He gave Eve to Adam. God made them so that they would be just right for one another. Both the man and the woman received all that they needed from the hand of God. In the garden that God made, they were never sick. Adam knew how it felt to trust God in every way. He knew how it felt to be blessed* by God. He knew how it felt to know that God was pleased with him.

God gave only one command to Adam and Eve. They could not eat from one tree in the middle of the garden where they lived. God told Adam to enjoy the food from every other tree in the garden. But the fruit from this one tree was not his to eat.

Why did God give Adam a command like this one? Think about it this way. Imagine you are walking down a path. You see a sign that says,

'DO NOT ENTER.'

A sign like that can be put there for two reasons. One, someone has something good there that they do not want you to have. The sign is a command to keep you from enjoying something. Or two, someone knows that there is danger ahead. The sign is a command to keep you from being hurt. God's command to Adam and Eve was like the second command. God knew that the fruit was not good for them. Bad things would happen to Adam and Eve if they ate from that tree. So, God said, 'No.' God did not give the command to take something from them. He gave the command to bless* them.

---

1. Psalm 16:11; Psalm 21:6

PART 2

Sin* *and* Law*

QUESTIONS 27 TO 62

question ——
027

Did Adam* and Eve* obey God and remain holy* and happy?

No, they did not obey. They chose to sin* against God.

Genesis 3:6–8

question ——
028

What is sin?

Sin is when we do not do what God tell us to do. And when we do what God forbids.

Romans 1:32 • James 2:10–11 • James 4:17 • 1 John 3:4

question ——
029

What does every sin deserve?

Every sin deserves the anger and punishment of God.

Deuteronomy 27:26 • Romans 1:18 • Romans 6:23
Ephesians 5:6

God is the one who created* all things. He created our first parents, Adam and Eve. God gave Adam and Eve all of the fruit in the garden to eat. And God made a rule for the man and the woman to live by. He kept only one thing from them. They were not to eat the fruit from one tree.

But Adam and Eve did not obey God. We use the word 'sin' to describe what they did. But it means more than to disobey. Sin is refusing to believe God. And it shows a failure to trust* God. Adam and Eve did not only break a rule. They believed the snake who came into the garden. He told them that God was keeping something good from them. And because they believed the snake, they doubted that God was good. And they doubted that God wanted the best for them. Sin means that they decided to stand against God. He was their Maker and Lord.* But they decided that they did not want to yield to God. They decided to stand against him. They imagined that they knew what was best for them better than God did. They thought that their way would be better than God's way.

> **Sin is refusing to believe God.**

Adam failed to keep God's one command. He did not give God the honor* that he deserved. He failed to give God glory.* He showed that he did not respect* God. When Adam sinned,* it meant that he did not consider God or his words of great worth.[1] It meant that he had stopped being loyal to God his maker. Adam did not only break a rule. When he sinned, he also broke a trust. And he broke a relationship.

Those things are also true when we sin. When we sin, we do not honor God. We show that we do not trust him. We show that we do not believe that God knows the best way. And we do not trust him to do what is best for us. We doubt that God is good. We doubt that he is wise. We want to please ourselves. And we believe that God is keeping something good from us. So, we go our own way and not God's way. We refuse to allow God to tell us what to do. And we say no to the one who made us. This is what our first parents did in the garden. And this is what we do when we sin.

God is holy. He is set apart from sin. When a person breaks a law,* there are always punishments that come with it. When we break God's law, he is the one who decides what the punishments will be.

God does not allow sin to go without punishment. The word that the scriptures* use to speak of God's anger for sin is the word 'wrath.'* Wrath is God showing that he has no pleasure when people sin. It is his justice* at work. He blesses* the ones who do right. He punishes those who do wrong.

God's wrath is not like human anger. When a man or woman become angry, they may lose control of themselves. They may do things that are not right or reasonable when they are angry. God's wrath is not like this. His anger is perfect and it is always right. He punishes sin. If he did not, he would not be holy.

Imagine that someone hurts you or takes something that belongs to you. You may go to court to ask the judge to punish that person. You want them to return what they took. Or you want them to be punished so that they will not hurt you again. If the judge knew that the person hurt you, but did nothing, he would not be a good judge. He would not be doing right. So, God would not be doing right if he did not judge those who do not obey his words.

Wrath is God's anger against sin and those who do sin. The wrath of God rests upon all who do not follow him.[2] Some day, God will judge all people.[3] He will bless* those who trust him. But God will punish all who do not trust him, for every evil* thing that they have done. He will pour out his wrath on 'all who do not know God and do not obey his good message.'[4]

---

1. Romans 1:21–24; 3:23
2. John 3:36
3. Psalm 9:7; Revelation 20:12
4. 2 Thessalonians 1:8

question —— 030

What was the sin* of our first parents?

They ate the fruit that God told them not to eat.

Genesis 2:16-17 • Genesis 3:6

question —— 031

Who tempted* them to sin?*

The Devil* tempted Eve* and she gave the fruit to Adam.*

Genesis 3:1-5 • John 8:44 • 2 Corinthians 11:3
Revelation 12:9

In the beginning, God made everything. He made the things that we can see and things that we cannot see. He made spirits called angels. When he made the earth, the angels were there shouting with joy. God made the angels to serve him and honor* him.

But some of the angels turned against God.[1] They became known as evil* spirits.* Their leader is Satan.*[2] He is also called the Evil One* or the Devil.[3] He and his evil spirits are still walking on the earth today. They work against God and God's plans.

In the book of Genesis, we only know that a snake spoke to our first parents. When we read further in the scripture*, we discover more. We find out that the person who spoke to Adam and Eve was the Devil. He came to Eve in the body of the snake.

Remember that God made Adam and Eve in his image. He blessed* them. He gave them a purpose. They represented God. They were God's partners to rule over and care for all that God had made. Everything that he gave them was good. And what he gave them was enough.

God gave Adam and Eve only one command.

'You must not eat from the tree that gives knowledge about good and evil. If you eat fruit from that tree, you will certainly die!'[4]

He gave them the command to protect them. So long as they obeyed God, they would enjoy God and all that God made for them.

But the Devil wanted Eve to stop trusting God. He wanted her to believe that what God had given her was not enough. And he wanted Eve to do what God had told her not to do. So, he lied to her. 'You will not surely die.'[5] And he tempted her to doubt God. He wanted her to desire the fruit that God had told her not to eat.

So, he told her that God was keeping her from something good. He said that God did not want them to eat the fruit because it would make them wise. If she would eat the fruit, she could 'be like God who knows good and evil.'[6] If she and Adam would eat the fruit, they could know things that only God knows.

And Eve believed Satan. So, she went to look at the tree. She saw that it was pleasing to look at. The fruit looked like it would be good to eat. For the first time, she began to desire the thing that God had kept from her.

Then Eve took the fruit. She gave some of the fruit to Adam. They both ate of the fruit. They both did what God had told them not to do.

This is the first time we read about the Evil One in the scriptures. But it is not the last time. We see him many times after this. He is always at work to do evil. He works to ruin all that God has made. He is the enemy of God. And he is the enemy of God's people. He works to destroy all that is good and right and beautiful.[7]

But God is still in control. He has more power than all of the spirits that he created.* One day, God will judge Satan and his evil spirits. Then he will throw them all into a fire that never goes out.[8]

---

1. 2 Peter 2:4; Jude 6; Revelation 12:7
2. Mark 3:22; Matthew 25:41;
   1 Timothy 5:15; Revelation 12:9
3. Matthew 13:19;
   2 Thessalonians 3:3; 1 John 5:18
4. Genesis 2:17
5. Genesis 3:4
6. Genesis 3:6
7. Acts 13:10; 1 John 3:7
8. Matthew 25:41; Revelation 21:10

question 032

What happened to the world when our first parents sinned?*

God spoke a curse* upon the ground. And death came into the world, just as God had warned* them.

Genesis 2:15-17 • Genesis 3:16-17

question 033

What happened to our first parents when they sinned?

God cast Adam* and Eve* out of the garden. They were no longer holy* and happy. Instead, they were sinful*- guilty, ashamed, and afraid.

Genesis 3:8-13 • 16-19 • 23

question 034

Because Adam sinned, what happened to everyone who lived after him?

Every person who was born after Adam and Eve was born sinful.

Psalm 51:5 • Romans 5:18-19 • 1 Corinthians 15:21-22

After Adam and Eve broke God's law* by eating of the fruit of the tree, everything changed. God came into the garden as he always did. But this time, Adam and Eve ran to hide from him. Now they were ashamed. They did not want God to see them. They were also ashamed to be seen by each other. So, they tried to cover themselves with leaves from the plants in the garden.

When they told God what they had done, God was not pleased with them. That was the first time they knew anything other than God's pleasure. They broke the one law God gave them. Now, they knew what it was like to feel guilt.* They felt shame. And they felt fear.[1]

Before they ate the fruit, they had all the food they needed. God gave them trees that he had planted. In the garden, the plants grew. There were no weeds or plants with sharp branches. Adam and Eve cared for the garden, and the work gave them joy. But God was not pleased with what they had done. So, after they ate the fruit, God cursed the soil. Now the soil would not give fruit so easily. Plants with sharp branches would grow. Weeds would grow among the good plants. And Adam would have to work very hard to grow food for his family.

Then God spoke a curse upon the snake. He said that the snake would crawl through the dust from that time on. The snake (Satan) and people would no longer be at peace* with each other.

God also spoke to the woman. He told her that she would still have many children. But now she would have pain when she had a child. Before, Eve and Adam were at peace with each other. Now they would struggle to see who would be in control. They would now blame one another for problems. And they would try to please themselves rather than please one another.

Then God put our first parents out of the garden. They would never be able to go back. And neither would anyone else.

Outside of the garden, their bodies would begin to grow old. Now their bodies could become sick. For the first time, they would know what it is to suffer. They would not live on and on. They would begin to die. Their bodies would grow tired. One day, they would die, and their bodies would return to the dust.

Now Adam and Eve knew about good and evil* in a new way. But it did not make them like God, as the snake had promised. Adam and Eve had done an evil thing. They had sinned against God. And sin* changed them. They were no longer able to hear God as they did before. Adam and Eve no longer wanted to love and obey God. They no longer thought the way God wanted them to think. They did not want to bow before God and honor* him as the one who created them. They did not care about what God wanted. They only wanted their own way.

Adam and Eve sinned. When they sinned, they changed. Because they sinned, they became sinners.* And they would pass this problem on to their children. From now on, people would do sinful things. They would do those sinful things because they are born as sinful people. They are born with a desire to sin.

Soon, Adam and Eve began to have children. And, when they did, their children were born with a desire to do wrong. They were just like their parents. Their first son even hated his brother and killed him. All of Adam and Eve's children would be born as sinners. And every child born after that would be a sinner too, just like Adam and Eve. As the years went by, the world would be filled with people. And every one of those people would do sinful things, just as Adam and Eve had done. The world did not work the way God had made it to work. The people who lived in the world did not think or act the way God had made them to act. They did not honor God. They became selfish. They did not want God to be in control of their lives. They did not love their neighbors* as much as they loved themselves.

So, because of what Adam did, the whole world became a broken place. Before people sinned, they knew God and understood him. After they sinned, they could not understand God in the same way. And they did not want to know God the way they once did. In fact, they no longer wanted to be close to God. Instead, they began to change the way they remembered God. Their minds and hearts* turned against him. They began to do evil instead of good. They even began to make other gods for themselves. They began to worship* the things God made instead of the God who made all things.

And the same is true of us. We (and everyone else) were born into a broken world. We are sinners. Like everyone else in the world, we follow our own sinful desires. We do the things that we want to do instead of what God wants us to do.[2] This is true of us and all of the children of Adam. The Scriptures* say it this way:

'There is not one person who is right with God, no one at all. There is no one who understands. There is not one who tries to find God. Everyone has turned away from God. They have all done wrong. Not one of them does what is good. No, not even one.'[3]

---

1. Genesis 3:7-11
2. Ephesians 2:3

3. Romans 3:10-13

035

Did God leave the world under a curse?* Did he leave people in their sin?*

No, God chose to rescue them. God promised to send a Savior.*

Matthew 1:21 • John 3:16-17 • 1 John 4:14

After Adam* and Eve* sinned*, they tried to hide from God. But people cannot hide from God. God is in all places. God knows everything.

So, when God came into the garden, he already knew what Adam and Eve had done. But he called for them so they would have to answer him. After they told God what they had done, they must have wondered what would happen to them.

Soon, Adam and Eve knew. They found out that God was not pleased. He allowed them to know the pain that their sin had caused. They felt shame. Now their lives would be full of trouble. All of their children would have trouble too. God sent them out of the garden that he had made for them. But they also learned that God shows mercy.* He does three things in Genesis 3 that show both mercy and grace.*

01 **First,** God returned to the garden to speak to them. Remember that God knew what they had done. God could have caused them to die at that moment. He would have been right to do so. If he had done that, he could have made another man and woman and started the world over again. But he did not do that. He came into the garden to meet with them. Although they had decided not to obey him, he returned to speak with them. That was an act of grace.

02 **Second,** God made clothes to cover their naked bodies. Adam and Eve had tried to cover their bodies with leaves from the trees. But this would not be enough for them to wear outside of the garden. So, 'The Lord* God made clothes out of animal skins for Adam and his wife to wear.'[1] God gave them what they needed to cover themselves. But, to do that, God had to take the life of some of the animals he had made. He would take the lives of these animals to cover the shame that sin had caused.

03 **Third,** God made two promises to Eve. He told her that she would continue to be able to have children. She would become the mother of every living person. And he made another promise as well. When he spoke the curse upon the snake, God said, 'I will make you and the woman hate each other. Your children and her children will be enemies. Her son will strike your head. You shall strike his heel.'[2] Satan* had used the snake to lie to Eve. So she now hated the snake. But, one day, God would send a child from Eve's family. He would defeat the snake and Satan, who had used it. The snake would hurt the son of the woman. But this son of Eve would press the snake's head under his foot.

When Eve heard this promise, she did not understand all that the promise meant. She did have many sons and daughters. She knew that each child came to her as a gift from God.[3] But she did not know that God would wait many years to bring the son who would achieve the promise. His name would be Jesus. He would be born of a woman without a man. He would be the seed of a woman. He would save his people from their sins.[4] One day, God would use him to overcome Satan. He would destroy Satan under his feet.[5]

The rest of the Bible* is the story of how God kept his promise.

---

1. Genesis 3:21
2. Genesis 3:15
3. Genesis 4:1; Genesis 4:25
4. Matthew 1:21
5. Romans 16:20; Revelation 12:9-10; Revelation 20:10

036

What is a covenant?*

A covenant is a serious promise between two or more persons.

037

What covenants did God make with the people of Israel?*

God promised to make Abraham's* family into a great nation. He promised to bless* all the nations through Abraham. God gave Moses* the law.* He promised to be with Moses and to bless Israel if they obeyed him and followed the laws he gave them. God promised David* that one of his sons would become a great king and rule forever. God promised that one day he would make a new covenant. He promised to forgive* people's sins* and to change people's hearts.*

Genesis 12:1-3 • Genesis 15 • Exodus 24:3-7
2 Samuel 7:16 • Jeremiah 31:31-34

A covenant is a serious promise. Two people can make these promises with one another. A master and a slave can make these promises. Or a covenant can be a promise made between a king and his people. The covenants God made with Abraham, Moses, and David are like the promises that a king might make with his people.

God made a covenant with Abraham. He told Abraham that he had chosen him. He would be Abraham's God. God would bless him. He would give Abraham a land of his own.[1] He would give him a son. This son would give Abraham a large family. And that family would become a great nation.[2] They would be more in number than the stars in the sky. God would bless this family. And God would also bless all nations[3] through Abraham. God made these promises to Abraham. He told Abraham's son Isaac* and his grandson Jacob* that this was their promise as well.[4]

Later, God made another covenant with Israel. He made this promise through Moses. He told Moses that he would be his God and the God of his people. He promised to make them a kingdom* of priests and a holy* nation.[5] He would take them out of the land of Egypt.* He would take them back to the land that God gave Abraham.

God did bring the people out of Egypt. He delivered them by doing many wonders there. After the people left Egypt, God gave laws to Moses. These laws told the people how to live as God's chosen people. When they obeyed these laws, the nations near them would see that Israel's God was great.

God promised the people that he would bless them if they obeyed him. He would watch over them. He would protect them from their enemies. They would be able to stay in the land that God had promised to Abraham.

But, if they did not follow the laws, the people would have many troubles. God would remove his blessing* from them. Their enemies would come into the land. And, if they did not turn back to follow God's laws, God would remove them from the land.[6]

When Moses told the people about this promise, they were happy. They promised to obey the laws that God gave them. They agreed to do all that God had told them.[7]

Many years later, God made a covenant with David. When he made this promise, God's people were living in the land that God promised to Abraham. David was their king. God told David that he would keep the promises that he made to Abraham and Moses. He would provide a place for his people.[8] Then he promised David that his son would follow him as king. This son would build a house to honor* God, a temple.*[9] Then he promised David something more. He promised that David's house and David's kingdom would last forever.[10] Another son from David's family would build a kingdom that would never end. We know now that this son would come many years later. He was Jesus, the son of David.[11]

God made another covenant as well. This promise was given to Abraham's family. But this promise was not for them alone. This was to be a new covenant. God would bring his people back from their wandering. He would then give them a new heart.[12] He would change them so that they would love him with 'all their soul* and live.'[13]

One of God's prophets* spoke of the new covenant this way. 'I will put my Spirit* in you. I will cause you to follow my laws and be careful to do what I tell you.'[14]

This new covenant did not begin until many years after the other covenants. God brought his old covenant to Israel through Moses. God would bring the new covenant through his son, Jesus. Jesus was the child of Abraham who came to bless all of the nations. Jesus was the one from the family of Israel who would keep all of the laws that God gave to Moses. Jesus was the son that God promised David who would be the King of Kings and Lord* of Lords.[15] When he died on the cross,* Jesus' blood was the sign that this new promise had begun.

Here is how another of God's prophets spoke of this covenant.

'The days are coming when God will make a new covenant with his people. When that day comes,' says the Lord, 'I will put my law into their minds. I will write it in their hearts. No one will need to teach his neighbor* or his brother to know the Lord. All of them will already know me. From the least important to the most important, all of them will know me,' says the Lord. 'I will forgive their sins and I will remember their sins no more.'[16]

The covenants that God made with Abraham, Moses, and David were good. This new covenant would be even better.[17]

---

1. Genesis 12:1; Genesis 13:14-18;
    Deuteronomy 30:1-10
2. Genesis 12:2
3. Genesis 12:3
4. Genesis 21:12; Genesis 26:3-4;
    Genesis 28:14-15
5. Exodus 19:6

6. Deuteronomy 28:1-68
7. Exodus 19:8
8. 2 Samuel 7:10
9. 2 Samuel 7:12-13
10. 2 Samuel 7:13,16
11. Matthew 21:9; Luke 1:32,69;
    Acts 13:34

12. Deuteronomy 29:4
13. Deuteronomy 30:1-5
14. Ezekiel 36:27
15. 1 Timothy 6:15
16. Jeremiah 31:31-34
17. Hebrews 7

question —— 038

What are the ten commands?

The ten commands are the words that God gave Moses* for the people of Israel.* God himself wrote the ten commands on two stone tablets.

Exodus 31:18 • Deuteronomy 9:10

question —— 039

What are those commands?

1. Do not put any other gods ahead of me.
2. Do not make for yourself an idol* nor worship* it.
3. Do not use the name of the Lord* your God in a wrong way.
4. Remember to keep the Sabbath* day holy.*
5. Give honor* to your father and mother.
6. Do not murder anyone.
7. Do not commit adultery.*
8. Do not steal.
9. Do not tell lies against your neighbor.*
10. Do not desire anything that belongs to your neighbor.

Exodus 20:1-17

These are the commands that God gave to Moses. They were part of God's covenant with his people. The scriptures* say that God wrote these words with his own hand. He gave them to Israel as a gift. This law* was the way that God would guide his people. God chose Israel and gave his commands to them because he loved them.[1] He wanted them to know how to please him. He wanted them to know how to be wise and live well with each other.

There were ten of these commands. But we should also remember that these commands are all a part of one law. When the people failed to do just one of the commands, they had broken the whole law.[2]

Most of the ten commands tell the people what they must NOT do. Why did God give his people commands like these? Think about it this way. Imagine you are walking down a path. You see a sign that says,

'DO NOT ENTER.'

That sign may be there for two reasons. One, someone has something good in that place that they do not want you to have. The sign is a command to keep you from enjoying something good. Or two, someone knows that there is danger ahead. This sign is a command to keep you from being hurt. God's Ten Commands to Moses are like the second example. God knew what was good for his people and what was not good for them. He knew that bad things would happen to them if they did not listen and they went their own way. So, God said, 'No.' God did not give the people the commands to take something from them. He gave them the commands to bless* them and keep them from harm. God is the one who made his people. God knew what was best for them. So, God did not give them the commands to put a burden upon them. He gave them these laws to guide them to what was good.

God also gave Israel these commands to show them his love. God did not give them the law to say, 'Do these things and I will accept you.' He had already chosen them to be his. He had already delivered them from being slaves in Egypt.* God gave them these laws to say, 'You are the people whom I have chosen. You are the people I have loved. Do these things and live.' He gave them the law to help them find joy. When the people understood the commands in this way, they found delight in obeying the law.[3] The men who wrote the Psalms* knew this. That is why they loved the law.[4] They called the commands good and right and beautiful.[5]

God gave these laws to Moses. But Jesus repeated them to the men and women who followed him. He wanted them to be guided by these laws too. They were to follow them as the way of wisdom. Jesus said that the law should not only guide their actions. Jesus wanted these laws to guide their hearts* as well.

Many years after God gave these commands, a man asked Jesus what command was the most important. He answered the man this way.

> 'Love the Lord your God with all your heart and with all your soul.* Love him with all your mind.' This is the first and most important command. And the second is like it. 'Love your neighbor as you love yourself.'[6]

Jesus said that when we obey the law as God intended, we show love. The commands show us how. The first four commands tell us how to show love for God. The last six commands tell us how to show love for our neighbors. If we love God, we will worship him alone. If we love our neighbors, we will not lie to them or steal from them. We will not speak words that would damage them. We will not be jealous of what they have. And we will want them to be loyal to their husbands or wives. If we love our neighbor, we show that love by how we act toward them.

Yes, it is possible to obey a law for a reason other than love. We may obey because we are afraid of punishment. But we cannot show true love for God without doing what he tells us to do. And we cannot show true love for our neighbor unless our actions toward them are loving.

---

1. Deuteronomy 4:37;
   Deuteronomy 7:6–8;
   Deuteronomy 10:15
2. James 2:9–11
3. Psalm 119:24; Psalm 119:35;
   Psalm 119:47; Psalm 119:77;
   Psalm 119:111; Psalm 119:162
4. Psalm 1:2; Psalm 119:97
5. Psalm 119
6. Matthew 22:37–39

question —— 040

What is the first command?

The first command is: Do not put any other gods ahead of me.

Exodus 20:3 • Isaiah 45:5-6

question —— 041

What does the first command teach?

The first command teaches us to worship* God only.

Psalm 44:20-21 • Matthew 4:10 • Revelation 22:8-9

The ten commands are the laws* God gave to his people, Israel.* They were part of the covenant* he made with them.

God gave the commands to Moses* when the people of God gathered near the mountain.[1] They saw a cloud covering the mountain. They saw lightning. They heard the noise of a storm. They heard God's voice as he spoke to Moses there.

But before God gave any commands, he begins the covenant with these words.[2] 'I am the Lord* your God. I brought you out of Egypt.* That is the land where you were slaves.' He says this so that the people will know who will give these commands. He is the Lord. He is the one God who made all things. Everything belongs to him. Even these people belong to him. He also chose them. These were his special people. He chose them when he made his promises to Abraham.* He told Abraham that he would become a great nation. Now this nation stands before him. He also is the God who has delivered them from Egypt. God is the one who made them. God is the one who rescued them. They are the people he has chosen.

Then God gives the first command. 'You will put no other god before me.'

When the people lived in Egypt, the people in that land followed many gods. But not one of these gods was the real God. In fact, they were not gods at all. The people in Egypt had created these gods in their minds. Then they made stories about these gods. They taught their children to believe in these gods. As many years went by, people came to believe that the gods were real. But the gods in Egypt were false gods. These gods could not protect them. These gods could not take care of them. There is only one true God. He is the Lord their God. This is why they must trust* him alone. They must worship him only. They must worship no other god.

God made our first parents, and each of us, so that only one thing can be first in our lives. Only one thing can be most important. Since the Lord alone is God, they must put nothing and no one before him. The people of God would be tempted* to follow other gods. They would remember the gods of Egypt. Or they would hear of new gods in the land where they were going. They would hear that another god could bring them good things. They would hear that another god could rescue them in times of trouble. But only the Lord God could do this for them. They must never turn away from him. God is telling them, 'Since I alone am God, you shall trust in me alone and no one else. You must not look to anyone else for the good things you enjoy. You shall not turn away to find shelter in anyone else in times of trouble. When you do you have begun to trust another god. That will only hurt you.'

> One day, many years later, a man asked Jesus a question.[3] 'Teacher,' he asked, 'which is the great command in the Law?' Jesus answered him and said, 'Love the Lord your God with all your heart* and with all your soul.* Love him with all your mind.' This is the first and great command.

That is the first command. God's people must never value anything more highly than they value God. They must never think that anyone else can do only what God can do. They must never trust anyone or anything more than they trust him. That would not honor* God. And that would only bring them trouble.[4]

---

1. Exodus 19:16-25
2. Exodus 20:1-2

3. Matthew 22:34-40;
Deuteronomy 6:5

4. Deuteronomy 28:15-19

042

What is the second command?

The second command is: Do not make for yourself an idol* or worship* it.

Exodus 20:4-6 • Deuteronomy 5:8-10

043

What does the second command teach?

The second command teaches me not to worship idols or images.

Isaiah 44:10-11 • Isaiah 46:5-9 • Acts 17:29

The second command helps to explain the first one. The first command says that God's people must worship him alone.

The second command says how they must worship him. They must not make an idol.

An idol is an image. People could make these images out of wood or stone or gold. The image could represent one of the false gods. Or an idol could represent the true God. In either case, God did not want his people to make an idol for themselves to use in worship.

There is only one God. There is only one true faith.* But the nations near God's people had many false gods.[1] The people of God would see these false gods and be tempted to follow them. Or they could be tempted* in another way. They could decide to worship the true God in the same way that the other nations worshipped false gods. The second command says no to both of those things.

God made the heavens and everything in them. He cannot be represented by something that looks like one of the things he has made. He made the heavens and the earth, the sea and the things under the sea. He is greater than all he has made. No idol can ever show all that is true about him.

Many years after Moses,* God sent prophets* to speak for him to the people. The prophets warned the people to stay away from idols. They told the people that God wanted to be their God. He wanted them to be his people. He wanted to be as close to them as a husband is close to his wife. So, they must be loyal to him. When a wife searches for another man to give herself to him, she is not loyal to her husband. What she does brings shame to their house. In the same way, when Israel* chose to follow a false god and worship an idol, the nation was not loyal to God. This would bring shame to the nation.[2] They would bring shame to God's name. The prophets warned them never to do this. They were God's own people. They were to be loyal to God and obey him completely.

When people follow a false god, they have no god at all. An idol is only the work of human hands. 'They have mouths, but they cannot speak. They have eyes, but they cannot see. They have ears, but they cannot hear. They have noses, but they cannot smell. They have hands, but they cannot feel. They have feet, but they cannot walk. They cannot make sounds come out of their mouths.'[3]

Yes, sometimes an idol may appear to have power. Honoring* an idol can sometimes seem to make a good thing happen. But this power does not come from a god. This power comes from Satan,* the Evil One* or the spirits* who follow him. Moses even says that when a person makes a sacrifice* to a false god, they bring a gift to an evil spirit.[4]

When people follow a false god, they have no god at all.

Evil spirits can make an idol seem as if it can do something for you. They can act like gods. They can even do wonders to fool the people who follow a false god. Evil spirits hate the true God. They always lead people away from God. If a person follows an idol it will always lead far away from God. That will always lead to trouble.

After God gives this command, he says. 'I, the Lord* your God, am a jealous God.'[5] Sometimes, the word jealous can describe someone who acts in an evil or selfish way. But God is neither evil or selfish. So, what does he mean?

First, God is not jealous of other gods. God is jealous for his own name, his own honor. If the people followed another god, the true God would lose the honor that belongs to him.

But he is also jealous in another way. God is jealous for his people. He wants what was best for them. He knows that if they follow any other god, they will suffer. They would become slaves again to these false gods. Soon, they would become the slaves of other nations as well. They would no longer have God's blessing.* Instead, they would face God's anger. That is why God spoke in such a strong way. He did not want them to forget.

God gave the command because he loved them. He gave these laws* to protect them. As long as they followed the commands, he would be their God. And they would be his people.

---

1. Romans 1:18-25
2. Jeremiah 3; Ezekiel 16; Hosea 2
3. Psalm 135:15-18
4. Deuteronomy 32:16-17
   compare 1 Corinthians 10:19-20
5. Exodus 20:5

question ——

044

What is the third command?

The third command says, 'Do not use the name of the Lord* your God in a wrong way.'

question ——

045

What does the third command teach?

The third command teaches us that we should not use God's name in a way that does not honor* him.

Isaiah 8:13 • Psalm 138:2 • Revelation 15:3-4

A person's name is important to them. In most cultures, people have more than one name. A person has a family name. They also have a name that their parents gave to them. A person's name tells people who they are and where they belong. Our names represent us. We can use a person's name in a way that honors them. Or we can use a person's name in a way that hurts them.

This command, like the first two, is about the way we worship* God. We must worship the true God and him alone. We must honor God and not worship an idol* or use an idol to worship the true God. And we must worship God by using his name in ways that honor him.

When God introduced the commands, he said, 'I am the Lord your God.' The word Lord is the most common name for God in the Bible.* When God met Moses* at the burning bush, he called himself, 'the Lord.' He said that he was, 'the God of Abraham,* Isaac,* and Jacob.* My name will always be the Lord. Call me this name for all time to come.'¹

The third command tells us that God's name is important to him too. This command tells us how we must use God's name. We must always value God's name. We must use his name with great care. But the third command is about more than the way that we speak.

When God chose Abraham's family, he made them his own people. Moses says that people would know Israel* as those who were 'called by the name of the Lord'² God's people take his name as their own. The way they act will affect the way people think and speak about God. The third command is not only about our words. The command is about our actions. We must act as people who are called by the name of the Lord.

What does this mean? We never do things that brings shame to his name. We must always act in ways that cause other people to think well of our God. We must never say that we are his people and live as if we do not know him. We must keep our promises. We must work hard and be honest in our work. We must do our work as if we are working for the Lord. If we are his people, we must do all that we do in ways that honor him. We must always live in ways that cause other people to think well of our God.

Many years after Moses, King David* wrote. 'O LORD our LORD. How great is your name in all of the earth. You have set your glory* in the heavens.'

God's name is not just a title.[3] God's name represents his holy* character. The way we use his name tells God how we feel about him. It shows other people how we feel about God as well.

Do we believe that God is powerful? Then we will not talk of him as if he were weak. We will never speak of him as if he could not do all that he wishes to do. Do we believe that he is righteous?* Then we will not accuse him of wrong. Do we believe that he is holy and true? Then we will never speak of him as if he is one who does not keep his word.

If we respect* God, we will use his name with respect. If we trust* God, we will act and speak as people who believe his promises.

This command also forbids us from using God's name for an evil* purpose. In the days after Moses, God spoke through men called prophets.* God would speak to them. Then they would tell the people, 'This is what the Lord says.' But there were also false prophets in those days. They used God's name when they spoke as well. But God had not spoken to them. They claimed to speak for God. But they did not speak the truth.

We must never claim to speak for God when God has not spoken to us. When we do this, we break the third command.

---

1. Exodus 3:12-15   3. Psalm 8:1
2. Deuteronomy 28:10

question ——

046

What is the fourth command?

The fourth command is: Remember to keep the Sabbath* day holy.*

Exodus 20:8-11 • Deuteronomy 5:12-15

question ——

047

What does the fourth command teach?

The fourth command teaches us to honor* God in our rest, in our work, and in our worship.*

Exodus 16:23 • Isaiah 58:13-14

The fourth command tells Israel* to remember the Sabbath day. They were to keep it as a holy day.

The word Sabbath means rest. The first time we hear about a day of rest is in the very first chapters of the Bible.* God made all things in just six days. When he finished the work, he did two things. He looked at all he had made and said, 'This is very good.' Then he rested.[1] He took the seventh day and rested from the work of making all things. God did not rest because he was tired. He rested to enjoy what he had made.

The next time we hear about Sabbath is just before God gave the ten commands to Moses.* God had brought the people out of Egypt.* They were in a desert place. There was not enough food there. There was not enough water there. The people were hungry. Their animals needed food and water too. So, God gave them food and water. He gave the people birds for meat. He gave them a special food called 'manna.' It was like bread. When they got up in the morning, they found the bread on the ground. All they had to do was gather it and eat it. But they could only gather enough for one day. If they gathered too much, the bread would spoil on the next day, and they could not eat it.

But there was one day that was different. On the sixth day, they were to gather enough manna for two days. Because, God said, 'The next day will be a sabbath.'[2] They were not to do any work on that day. No manna would be on the ground on that day either. That day, they were to rest. They were to remember that God had brought them out of Egypt. They were to remember that God had set them apart from all other people on the earth.

The next time we hear about Sabbath, is here, in the fourth command. The command became part of the covenant* that God made through Moses. From that day on, the people were to do their work on the first six days of each week. But on the seventh day, the Sabbath day, no one was to work. The fathers and mothers could not work. Their sons and daughters could not work. Their servants could not work. Even their animals had to rest. This day was holy.[3]

But one day of rest in seven was not the end of God's Sabbath commands. God told them that the seventh year was also holy for them. In that year, they could not plant or gather a harvest. They were to rest. They were to allow the land to rest too. And like the first sabbath, God would provide enough food for them. God would bless* their crops. What they would grow in the sixth year would be enough for the next year too.

The Sabbath was a sign[4] to Israel. It reminded them of the covenant God had made with them. God gave them the Sabbath to remind them that they were his chosen people. They were the people that God delivered from Egypt.[5] He had brought them out of Egypt so they were no longer slaves. He set them apart for himself.[6] They were not like any other nation. No other nation had a Sabbath rest as they did.

Now Israel had to remember this day in all that they did. They bought and sold. They planted and gathered the harvest. They made things and traded things. But they always had to remember that the Sabbath was coming.

We do not keep the Sabbath today as the people of Israel did. But the fourth command reminds us of many important things. God has made us. God has set us apart for himself. We are God's chosen people.[7] And just as God rescued Israel, Jesus* has rescued us. We are no longer slaves to our sin.*[8] For we have believed the promise of Jesus.

GOD HAS SET US APART.

'Come to me, all of you who are tired. Come, all of you who are carrying a heavy load. I will give you rest.'[9]

Now we are to set every day apart for God. Whether we buy or sell, plant or gather, work or rest, we are to do them all for God's glory.* Not only that, but we also are to have hope.* Another time of Sabbath is in our future. One day, Jesus will return. He will rule as Lord* and King in a New Heaven* and a New Earth. All who know him will rest. There will be no more pain or death. There will be no more guilt* or fear or shame. Our souls* and bodies will have found complete joy and rest in Jesus.

1. Genesis 2:1-3
2. Exodus 16:1-36
3. Exodus 20:10
4. Exodus 31:13; Ezekiel 20:12,20
5. Deuteronomy 6:15
6. Exodus 31:12-13
7. 1 Peter 2:9
8. Romans 6:16
9. Matthew 11:28

question — 048

What is the fifth command?

The fifth command is: Give honor*
to your father and your mother.

Exodus 20:12 • Deuteronomy 5:16

question — 049

What does the fifth command teach?

The fifth command teaches us to
love and to obey our parents.

Proverbs 1:8 • Ephesians 6:1-3 • Colossians 3:20

Jesus said there are two commands in the law* that are the most important in life. The first command is, 'Love God with all of your heart.'* The second command is, 'Love your neighbor* as yourself.' These two commands work together. They give us a way to think about the 10 commands that God gave to Moses.* The first four commands teach us how to love God. The last six commands show us how to love other people.

If I am to love other people, I must start by showing love and honor to the people in my own family.

The fifth command tells us to 'give honor' to our parents.

The word 'honor' means to give respect* to someone. It means to act in a way that brings joy and not shame. When we honor our father and mother, we value them. We show them respect.

The Family

When God made Adam* and Eve,* he told them to fill the earth with children. They were to bring a family into the world. God gave parents the responsibility to care for their children.

Our parents are the first people we know. They are the first people who protect us and care for us. They are to provide for our needs. They teach us the right way to live. Our father and mother teach us about God. They tell us the stories about God and show us how to know him and follow him. The family is the place where children learn about authority. We honor our father and mother when we obey what they teach us.

Honoring Other People

When children learn to show respect to parents, they learn an important lesson. They understand they are under authority. Someone can tell them what to do and they must obey them. Parents are the first people to have authority over us. But they are not the only people.

The family is a part of a larger group. Our family is part of a community.* Our community is a part of a nation.

We honor our parents. We respect our community. We value the nation we live in because God has given his authority to people in that nation. All the families in the nation were to obey the people in authority.

But the leaders in the nation are under authority too. They are under the authority of God.

The Fifth Command Comes with a Promise

God gave all of the commands to benefit us. In the New Testament,* Paul* says the fifth command is the first command with a promise. This command is given by God for our blessing.* When we follow this command, we will live a long and good life. When we honor our father and mother, it pleases God. Good families build good communities. Good communities build a good nation. We first learn how to live this way in our family.

The family is the first to care for a child. The family is the first place a child learns what is right and wrong. God gave our parents authority over us. They are to care for us. So, we first learn how to follow our parent's authority. We learn that our parents are under authority as well. They submit* to the rules of a community. But most of all, they submit to God's authority above all. Good parents teach us to do this too.

What is the sixth command?

The sixth command is: Do not murder anyone.

Exodus 20:13 • Deuteronomy 5:17

What does the sixth command teach?

The sixth command teaches us not to hate other people or take away someone's life.

Genesis 9:6 • Matthew 5:21-22 • 1 John 3:15

The sixth command tells Israel,*
'You must not murder.'

God gave this command to each person under the covenant.* This command does not speak about rulers who may lead an army or must act as a judge. It does not speak about war. It does not speak to a judge who must take someone's life to punish them for doing wrong. There are other places in the law* that speak about those matters.

No person should take away the life of another person.

God gave our first parents life. He is the one who gives all life. Because life is a gift from God, we must value life as God does. So, the life of each person is sacred.* The word sacred means 'of great value and important.' The word speaks of a thing that is set apart by God. It belongs to God. It is to be devoted to him and him alone. He is the one who created* all that lives. God is the one who gives life. He is the only one who may take life away.

Human life is sacred to God for another reason. People – both men and women, are made in God's image. Long before God spoke to Moses,* God spoke to a man named Noah.* This is what God said to Noah. 'For sure, I will take the life of ... every person for taking a life. I will punish every man's brother for taking the life of man. Whoever takes the life of a man will have his life taken. For God made man to be like him.'[1] God made men and women 'in his own image.'[2] When God made Adam* and Eve,* he made them to reflect who he is in certain ways. God made nothing else that could do this in the same way.[3]

For this reason, we must value the lives of all men and women. We must never treat anyone as if their life has no value.

This command did not only mean that one person must not murder another person. God also told Moses that people must take great care to protect the lives of other people. If a man knows

**God cares about
what we think and
how we feel.**

that another man is in danger, he must warn the man. If I know that a man is going somewhere or doing something that can hurt him, I must warn him. I must act to save his life.[4]

In the law that God gave Moses, a man who murders another man must die. Sometimes, if a person broke a command, they could pay money as a punishment. Sometimes, they could run away and hide in a special town to avoid punishment. But for murder, no payment could be made.[5] For murder, there was no place to hide. When a man or woman murders someone, God sees them. And God will judge them.

Jesus* talked about this command many times. But he did not only speak about the act of murder. He spoke against the things that cause one person to murder another. He did tell people that they must not murder. But he also told them that they must not be angry with one another. He told them that they must not hate one another. 'Here is what I tell you. Do not be angry with your brother. Anyone who is angry with his brother will be judged.'[6]

Jesus said that if we have hate in our heart for someone, we break this command. 'Everyone who hates his brother is a murderer.'[7]

God is not only interested in what we do. He cares about what we think and how we feel. Jesus wanted people to know this. When we allow anger and hate to stay in our hearts*, that does not please God.

Murder always starts in the heart. That is the place where it must be stopped as well. Jesus told us that we must avoid hate and anger. Instead, we must love our neighbors.* Not only that, we must even love our enemies. But we cannot do this without God's help.

The laws that God gave to Moses could not change people's hearts. Only God can change the heart. This is why Jesus came. He came to bring a new covenant that would change people's hearts.[8] For unless God changes our hearts, we can never truly obey his commands.

1. Genesis 9:5-6
2. Genesis 1:26-27; Genesis 5:1
3. See Questions 21 & 22
4. Exodus 21:28-29
5. Number 35:31
6. Matthew 5:21-22
7. 1 John 3:15
8. Jeremiah 31:31-34

question — 052

What is the seventh command?

The seventh command is: Do not commit adultery.*

Exodus 20:14 • Deuteronomy 5:18

question — 053

What does the seventh command teach?

The seventh command teaches us that we must not have sex with someone who is not our husband or wife.

Matthew 5:27-28 • Ephesians 5:3-4

Many of the commands that God gave to Moses* tell us what not to do. We must not worship* other gods. We must not murder. And now, we must not commit adultery.

But all of the commands also tell us what we should do to please God. For example, the first command tells us that we must be devoted to God. The second command says that we must be loyal to God. The third command says that we must respect* God in the way we speak.

This command tells us that we must be faithful* to our husband or wife. We must be loyal to them.

Just as life is sacred,* sex is sacred too. God made the first man and woman so they could produce children.[1] He made their bodies so they fit together. In this way, they would feel pleasure. They would become as one.

God gave sex to our first parents as a gift. But they were to enjoy the gift only with each other. Sex was to be enjoyed between one man and one woman. And the man and the woman were to be married to one another. They were not to give their body to anyone else. They were not to try to make another man or woman desire them. And they were to be loyal to their husband or wife as long as they lived.

The nations near the place where Moses lived did not act this way. They did not think that sex was a gift from God. They acted as if it were nothing. They believed that it was just another desire. When you are hungry, you eat. When you are tired, you sleep. So, when you want sex, you satisfy that desire. It did not matter how or with whom.

But God wanted his people to be different. He did not want them to act as if sex was nothing. He wanted them to be loyal to their husband or wife. All through the pages of scripture,* God reminds his people of this. In the book of Proverbs,* God called men to be loyal to their wives. Again and again, Proverbs warns them to avoid adultery.[2]

When Jesus* came, he spoke of this command as well. But he did not only warn against adultery. Jesus warned against the desires that would lead them to commit adultery. He said that a man must not look at a woman with desire for her. If he has a desire to be with her, he has already broken the command. He has committed adultery with her in his heart.[3] Jesus tells people that they must avoid these desires. They must do anything to stop themselves from adultery.[4]

Jesus tells us that all sin* first begins in our hearts.*[5] Before I break the commands with my body, I break them in my heart.[6] So we must turn away from these evil* desires.[7]

Sex is for marriage. It is only for married people.[8] We must give our bodies to our husband or wife. Our bodies belong to them and them alone.[9] We must not try to make anyone desire us in a way that leads them to break this command.

When we break this command, we do great harm. We hurt our husband or wife. We harm the person whose body we take. We hurt ourselves. We hurt our relationship with God. This is why we must avoid adultery no matter what it costs us.

Jesus tells us that all sin* first begins in our hearts.

One day, some men brought a woman to Jesus.[10] They said that they caught her in the act of adultery. They wanted Jesus to judge her. They wanted Jesus to tell them to throw stones at her so that she would die. But Jesus asked them a question instead. 'Are any of you without sin? Then you may throw the first stone.'

They all walked away.

So, Jesus told her that she could leave too. But he told her to 'go and sin no more.' Jesus was not saying that her adultery did not matter. She did deserve to die for this act of adultery. But Jesus forgave her. How could he do this?

Not many days in the future, Jesus would die on a cross.* On that cross, he would take the punishment that she deserved upon himself.[11]

1. Genesis 2:18-24
2. Proverbs 4:23, 27;
   Proverbs 6:20-7:27
3. Matthew 5:28

4. Matthew 5:29-30
5. Matthew 15:19
6. Colossians 3:5-6
7. Romans 13:14

8. Hebrews 13:4
9. 1 Corinthians 7:4
10. John 8:3-11
11. 1 Peter 2:24

054

What is the eighth command?

The eighth command is: Do not steal.

Exodus 20:15 • Deuteronomy 5:19

055

What does the eighth command teach?

The eighth command teaches us that we must not take things that belong to other people.

Exodus 23:4 • Proverbs 21:6-7 • Ephesians 4:28

When God made men and women, he gave them work to do. He made the world so that people could eat the things they grow. They could make things from the work of their hands. They could have things that belong to them. God gave this command to protect the things that people own.

God wants us to work for what we desire. This work is the way that we can get what we need. When we take something that does not belong to us, we steal. When we steal, we sin.* We break God's command. But we also sin against the person we steal from.

This is the eighth command from the Law* of Moses.* But this is not just a law for Moses and his people. All people know that it is wrong to steal. If we cannot protect the things that we own, we are not safe. We cannot feed our family. We cannot provide clothes for our family. No one wants people to steal from them. No community* can live in peace* without this command.

The first people to take what did not belong to them were our first parents. Eve* saw the fruit that God had said she could not have. God had not given this tree to them for food. But Eve wanted it. She took the fruit that did not belong to her.

When we break one command, we break other commands as well.

Here is an example. If I commit adultery,* I break the sixth command. But I also break the eighth command. I take something that does not belong to me. When I break one command, I also break many other commands.

Jesus* spoke about this command many times.[1] He said that the sin of stealing begins in the heart.*[2] This is where all sin begins.[3] Jesus said that Satan,* the Evil One,* is a thief.[4] God hates the sin of stealing.[5]

The men who followed Jesus hated stealing as well. They taught that a person who steals must stop.[6] If they do not, they will never be part of God's kingdom.*[7]

Moses told people to give part of what they had to God. These gifts would pay for the work of the temple* and the priests. When they did not give these gifts to God, the prophets* said that they had stolen from God.[8] They broke the eighth command.

We also steal when we do not work hard for our employer. When we do not do the work that we are paid to do, we steal.

If a person works for us, we should not make them wait for what we owe them. We must be honest and pay them for the work that they have done.[9]

Imagine that I want to sell something that is broken. If I do not tell the person buying it about it, I have lied. And I am also a thief. I steal because I take money from someone and do not give them something of value in return. I must be honest about the value of what I am selling.[10]

When we break one command, we break other commands as well.

We can steal from someone in other ways. We can lie and say bad things about a person. If we do this and people think bad thoughts about them, we break the eighth command. We have taken away their good name. Or, imagine that a person has done something very good. They deserve praise* for what they have done. When we fail to praise that person, we keep something from them that belongs to them.[11]

Stealing can lead to other crimes. It makes the world an unsafe place. The person who is the victim of stealing loses their property. But the thief loses something too. He loses his good name. He may even lose his life. Under the law that God gave to Moses, a man caught stealing could be put to death.[12]

This is not just a law for Moses and his people. This is a law for all people. All people know that we cannot live together and feel safe when people steal.

1. Matthew 19:18; Mark 10:19; Luke 18:20
2. Matthew 15:19–20
3. James 1:14–15
4. John 10:10
5. Joshua 7:1
6. Ephesians 4:25–28
7. 1 Corinthians 6:9–10
8. Malachi 3:7–8
9. Deuteronomy 24:15; Leviticus 19:13; Jeremiah 22:13; James 5:4
10. Proverbs 11:1; Proverbs 20:23
11. Romans 13:7
12. Deuteronomy 24:7

question 056

What is the ninth command?

The ninth command is: Do not tell lies against your neighbor.*

Exodus 20:16 • Deuteronomy 5:20

question 057

What does the ninth command teach?

The ninth command teaches us to be honest and to tell the truth.

Psalm 15:23 • Proverbs 12:17 • 1 Corinthians 13:6

People sometimes say, 'A man is only as good as his word.' What do they mean when they say that? 'You can judge whether a man is good or bad by how well he keeps his promises.' We cannot trust* a person who does not tell the truth. A person who lies can do great harm.[1]

Remember that the first four commands teach us how to love God. The last six commands tell us how to love our neighbors.[2] If we love our neighbor, we will not tell lies about them.

We break the ninth command when we lie. But there are other ways to break the command as well. One way is to boast. We say things about ourselves that are not entirely true. We say something to make us seem smarter or stronger or wiser than we are.

Sometimes, a person will lie to get more money. They will say things that are not true about what they want to sell. They may gain money that way, but they cannot earn a good conscience that way.[3]

Slander is another way we break the ninth command. We tell stories about someone that are not true. Or we tell only part of the truth about someone. We want people to think badly about that person. God is not pleased with this. He tells us that a person who speaks in this way is a fool.[4]

There are many reasons people lie. Sometimes we lie because the truth would bring us shame. We make a mistake. We do something bad, so we do not want people to know what we have done. We care too much about what other people will think of us. We are proud. So, we lie so we will not feel shame.

The Bible* tells us that God always keeps his promises. We can always trust that what he says is true. The scriptures* tell us that God cannot lie. We can always believe what he says.[5] The God who made us is the 'God of truth.' He always tells the truth in his speech and his actions.[6] So, if we are to be his people, we must be honest.

Lying starts in the heart.*[7] We begin lying early in our lives. David* says that we are born speaking lies.[8] Because God knew that this was a problem, he gave his people this command. He wanted them to be people who tell the truth.

The Evil One* was the first person to tell a lie. He told Eve* that God did not mean what he said. God had told Adam* not to eat from the tree in the middle of the garden. 'If you eat from that tree,' God said, 'You will certainly die.' But the Evil One told her a lie. He said that she would not die. Instead, if she ate from the tree, she would be like God.[9] Because the Evil One lied and Eve listened, God was not pleased. Adam and Eve had to leave the place God made for them. And every bad thing that we know about today came into the world. Now, the Bible says that all people tell lies, just like the Evil One.[10]

Many years after God gave Moses* this law,* the prophets* reminded the people of the command.

'Speak the truth to one another. Make right and wise decisions in your courts. Do not make evil plans against one another. When you promise to tell the truth, do not lie. Many people love to do that. But I hate all these things, says the Lord.'*[11]

If we continue to lie and do not speak the truth, God will not welcome us to be with him.[12]

People who follow God are people who tell the truth.

---

1. Proverbs 25:18
2. Mark 12:30-31
3. Proverbs 21:6
4. Proverbs 10:18

5. Titus 2:1; Hebrews 6:19
6. Isaiah 65:16
7. Matthew 15:18-19
8. Psalm 58:3

9. Genesis 3:1-6
10. John 8:44; Psalm 116:11
11. Zechariah 8:16-18
12. Revelation 21:7-8

question —— 058

What is the tenth command?

The tenth command is: Do not desire anything that belongs to your neighbor.*

Exodus 20:17 • Deuteronomy 5:21

question —— 059

What does the tenth command teach?

The tenth command teaches us to be content* with what we have.

Philippians 4:11 • 1 Timothy 6:6 • Hebrews 13:5

The tenth command talks about our desires. 'You must not want to have your neighbor's house. You must not want his wife. And you must not want his men and women servants. You must not want his cattle or his donkeys. You must not want to have anything that belongs to another person.'[1]

But what does the command mean? The Bible* does not say that all desires are bad. God promised to bless* his people if they obeyed his covenant.* They were to desire these blessings* from God. It is not wrong for us to desire food[2] or drink[3] or sleep.[4] It is not wrong for us to desire to have children[5] or to live in a good place.[6] But when we desire something so much that we hurt our neighbor to get it, we break the tenth command.

For example, it is not wrong for me to admire something that my neighbor has. I may even wish that I had it as well. But it would be wrong if I wanted to take that thing. And it would be wrong if I became angry with my neighbor because he or she had something I did not have. A desire that makes me jealous of someone else is an evil* desire.

I can also break this command in another way. God tells his people to be content, to be happy with what they have.[7] But sometimes, I have a desire for things that I do not have. I may want these things because I am not content with what God has given me. I forget that God has given me all that I have. I doubt that he will provide for my needs. When that happens, the things I desire can become more important to me than God. Paul* says that those kinds of desires are like idolatry.* Why does he say that? Because anything that I love more than I love God becomes an idol* to me.

Jesus* said that when we break the commands, there is a problem with our hearts.* Before we act in a wrong way on the outside, there is already something wrong on the inside.

Before I murder someone, I first have a desire to hurt that person. Jesus says that our anger can lead us to have this evil desire.[8] Before I commit adultery,* I first have a desire to be with someone else's husband or wife. Before I steal, I want something that belongs to someone else. The tenth command makes this clear to us. When we have a desire that will lead us to break God's commands, that is a sinful* desire. Sin* always begins in the heart.

Jesus once said. 'A good man says good things. These come from the good that is in his heart. An evil man says evil things. These come from the evil that is in his heart.' Sin always begins on the inside of a person. The Old Testament* speaks about a person's heart as well.[9] God told Israel that they must love him with all of their heart.[10] We cannot always see when someone breaks this command. But we almost always know when we break it.

> **To be content is to be happy with what we *have*.**

God promised to care for his people Israel.* But sometimes, they forgot his promises. They forgot all of the good things God had done for them. Then, they stopped trusting him. They even began to follow other gods. Why did they do this? They did it because they loved what they wanted more than they loved God.

When we forget God's promises, we stop trusting him too. Then we will want things that God has not given us. Those desires can lead us away from God. Each time that happens, we break the tenth command.

The last six commands help us know how to be good to our neighbors. We will not be good to our neighbors if we want what they have for ourselves.

*To be content is to be happy with what we have. To know that what God has given us is enough.

---

1. Exodus 20:17
2. Matthew 4:2
3. John 19:28-29
4. Luke 8:23
5. Genesis 30:22-23; 1 Samuel 1:17; Psalm 127:3-5
6. Proverbs 24:27
7. 2 Corinthians 9:8; Philippians 4:11; 1 Timothy 6:6-8; Hebrews 13:5
8. Matthew 5:21-24
9. Deuteronomy 11:18
10. Deuteronomy 6:5-6

question —— **060**

Did the Jewish* people obey the laws* that God gave to Moses?*

No. They broke God's law and God punished them, as he had warned them.

Deuteronomy 9:12 • Ezekiel 39:23

question —— **061**

Can any person keep God's commands in every way?

Adam* did not obey God. Since that time, no mere man has been able to keep God's commands in every way.

Ecclesiastes 7:20 • Romans 3:23 • James 2:10

God had made a covenant* with Abraham.* He made many promises to Abraham and his family. He promised Abraham that he would give them a land of their own. He promised to make them a great nation. He promised to be with them and guide them. He promised that they would bring a blessing* to all of the other nations.[1]

Many years after Abraham died, Abraham's children became slaves in Egypt.* They lived there for 400 years and they could not leave. But God rescued them from Egypt.[2] Moses became their leader. God gave Moses the ten commands to guide the people. The commands told them how to live to honor* God. And God made promises to the people. If they obeyed the commands, God promised to bless* them. But if they did not obey, God would punish them. They would lose the blessings God had offered to them.

The ten commands were the rules that God gave them. He gave them the commands to bless them. If they lived the way the commands told them to live, their nation would be great. They would live in peace.* The people were happy to hear these commands. And they all promised to obey them. Moses was to help them understand the commands.

The children of Abraham did become a great nation. David* became their king. They lived in the land God gave to Abraham. But they did not obey God. Again, and again, they turned away. They did not obey the commands. They did many things that did not please God. God would correct them. God even sent prophets* to tell them to obey the covenant again. But they did not turn back to God. They did not listen to the prophets. They even began to follow other gods.[3]

Many years after Moses and David had died, God punished his people. God brought a great nation to fight against them. This nation would take many of the people away from their land. For many years, Abraham's children would have to live in a strange land. God sent prophets to them. The prophets told them that God was not pleased with them. They had broken their promises to God. But God had not broken his promises to them. If they would obey him again, he would bring them home to their land. And God did bring them back to their land. But even then, the people did not do what they had promised.

What was wrong with Abraham's children? Why did they keep doing wrong things?

They did not obey God because they had the same problem that every person has. They were sinful.* From the very beginning, our first parents chose not to obey God. When they did this, sin* entered our world. Adam and Eve* chose to sin. They did not want to listen to God. They did not want to obey the one command he had given them. They believed the Evil One.* They doubted that God was good. They turned away from the God who made them.[4]

Ever since then, every person is born in sin. David says,

**'I have done bad things since I was born.
I have wanted to sin since the day of my birth.'[5]**

Sin is the wrong things people do against God and other people. When we do not follow the rules that God made, we sin. When we do not do what God wants us to do, we sin. All people are sinful. Something is broken inside of us. We are born with bad desires. And we choose to follow those bad desires.

No person, born of a man and a woman, has ever obeyed God in every way.[6]

That is why the scriptures* says,

**'It is true that there is no one on earth
who does only what is right and never sins.'[7]**

---

1. Genesis 12:1-3
2. Exodus chapters 1 to 14
3. Jeremiah 11:10

4. Genesis 3:1-24
5. Psalm 51:5
6. Romans 3:10-12

7. Ecclesiastes 7:20

What do the ten commands show us?

The ten commands teach us that God is holy* and good. They teach us how to show love for God and for our neighbor.* They show us that we are sinful* and do not obey God. They show us that we need a Savior.*

Ecclesiastes 12:13 • 1 Timothy 1:8-9 • Romans 3:20
Romans 5:13 • Romans 7:7-11 • Galatians 3:19-24

If I go to another country, I need to learn the laws* there. The laws tell me what is right and wrong. They also tell me something about the people who made those laws. They tell me what they think is important. The laws tell me what the people value. They tell me what they think I should do to be a good citizen.

Why did God give us the Ten Commands? What do the commands show us?

First, the laws of God show us what God is like. They tell me about the God who made those laws. They tell me what God loves. They tell me what he hates. The commands tell me that God wants people to love him. And he wants people to care for each other. God's laws are wise because God is wise. His laws are good because he is good. God's laws can be trusted because God always keeps his promises. His laws are true because he always tells the truth.

The commands also help us know how to show our love to God. Jesus said, 'If you love me, keep my commands.'*[1] When we look at the Ten Commands, we learn what pleases God. We also learn what does not please him. If we love God, we will want to do the things that please him.[2] We show our love for him when we do what he commands.

The Ten Commands also protect us from evil.* In most places, when I break the law, I will be punished. So, laws protect us. Sometimes a person wants to do wrong. But they do not do wrong because they do not want to be punished. Some people will only do good if someone makes them do good. That is one reason God gave the Ten Commands to Israel.* The commands helped them live together in peace.*

The Ten Commands also help us to know things about ourselves. James* tells us that the law is like a mirror.[3] Look at it one way, and I see how perfect and holy God is. Look at it another way, and I see how much I am not like him. I can see what I should do. But I also see what I have not been doing. A mirror helps me see if my face is dirty. A mirror helps me see places that I need to clean. So, when I see myself in the mirror of God's commands, I can see my sins.*4 The law helps me see that there are things in my life that need to change.

The commands God gave Moses* are good and right. But there is one thing the commands could not do. The law could not change a person's heart.* We cannot obey the law and become right with God.5 We break the commands. We want things that do not please God. And we cannot seem to stop. It is like we have become slaves to our sin, and we cannot get away.6

How can we ever be right with God?

God must do something for us that we cannot do for ourselves. What we need is someone to save us. The good news is – God did send a Savior.7

1. John 14:15
2. Psalm 19:7–11
3. James 1:22–25
4. Romans 3:20; Romans 4:15;
   Romans 5:13
5. Romans 3:20
6. Romans 7:14; Galatians 3:21–24
7. Luke 2:11; 2 Timothy 1:9–10;
   Titus 2:13; 1 John 4:14;
   Jude 1:24–25

———

*WE SHOW
OUR LOVE FOR
GOD WHEN WE
DO WHAT HE
COMMANDS.*

———

PART 3

Christic *and* Salvation*

question 063

Who is the Savior*?

The only Savior of sinners* is the Lord* Jesus* Christ.*

Luke 2:11 • Acts 4:11-12 • 1 Timothy 1:15

question 064

Who is Jesus Christ?

Jesus Christ is the eternal* Son of God.

John 1:1 • John 1:14 • John 1:18 • John 3:16-18
Galatians 4:4 • Colossians 1:15-18 • Hebrews 1:1-3
1 John 5:20

Before Jesus was born, an angel* came to a young woman named Mary.* The angel told Mary that she was going to have a son. Her son, Jesus, would be the Savior, Christ the Lord. So, the scriptures* often speak of Jesus in this way; the Lord Jesus Christ.

The angel told Mary to name the baby, Jesus. 'You will call his name Jesus, for he will save his people from their sins.*'¹ The name Jesus means 'God saves.'

The word 'Christ' is the word Jesus' followers* used to say that he was the Messiah.* The name means 'the one whom God has chosen.' God had promised his people to send someone to rescue them. This person would be the child God promised to Abraham.* He would be the ruler who would come from the tribe* of Judah.* He would be a prophet* like Moses.* He would be the king that would come from David's* family. God's people called this promised Savior the Messiah. In the language of Jesus' day, they called this promised Savior, the Christ.

The scriptures also speak of Jesus by the name, 'Lord.' This word means a master or ruler. That is the name that the Jews* used for God.

So, when we call Jesus the Lord Jesus Christ, we are saying many things about him. He is the son born to Mary. He is a man of flesh and blood like other men. He has taken on our nature. When we call him Lord, we say that he is God, our ruler, and master. When we call him the Christ, we say that he is the promised Savior, the Messiah, the one God's people had been waiting for.

The New Testament* also speaks of Jesus as the Son of God. What do the scriptures mean by this? We must read all of the scriptures with care to find the answer. Here are the answers that we find.

01 **First,** the Son of God is eternal. That means that the Son of God had no beginning and no end. That means that the Son of God existed before God made the world.[2] In fact, the scriptures tell us that he was the one who created* all things.[3] The Son of God was not created because he is God.

02 **Second,** the eternal Son of God did not always have a body. But God worked a miracle* in the body of Mary. The Holy Spirit* of God caused a child to grow in Mary's body. The Son of God took on a body as he grew in the body of a woman. He took on a human nature, a human mind, and a human will as well. He was born in the same way other human babies are born. He grew up to become the man that we know as Jesus.[4] He lived in this body. He died in this body. He rose from death in this body.

03 **Third,** Jesus spoke of God as his Father. The Jews who heard him knew what Jesus was saying when he did this. They knew that Jesus was saying that he was equal with God.

One time, the Jews became very angry when Jesus called God his Father. They were so angry that they picked up stones. They wanted to throw these stones at Jesus to kill him.

Jesus asked them, 'If I am doing my Father's work, why do you want to kill me?' The Jews said, 'We are not going to throw these stones because you did a good work. We are going to stone you because you said a very evil thing. You are only a man. But you say that you are God.'[5]

Jesus is the one-of-a-kind, eternal Son of God. He is one with God the Father in a way that no one else has ever been. That is why John* called Jesus 'the one and only' Son of God.[6] All that God is, Jesus is. He has always been. He will always be.

Yes, this is hard to understand. And yet, the New Testament says this again and again. Jesus is the Lord from heaven.* He shows us God in such a way that, if we have seen Jesus, we have seen the Father.[7] Jesus did things that only God could do. He gave people life and raised the dead.[8] He forgave people of their sins.[9] And one day he will sit as the judge of the whole world.[10]

———

JESUS IS THE ONE-OF-A-KIND, ETERNAL SON OF GOD.

———

1. Matthew 1:21; Luke 1:31; Luke 2:21
2. John 16:28; John 17:5
3. John 1:3; Colossians 1:16
4. John 1:1-12; Hebrews 1:1-6
5. John 10:31-33
6. John 3:16-18; 1 John 4:9
7. John 14:6-11
8. John 5:21; John 11:25
9. Mark 2:5-7
10. Matthew 25:31-4

Why did God send His Son into the world?

God sent his Son into the world because he loved us. He sent his Son because he is a God of mercy* and grace.*

Psalm 103:8-11 • John 3:16-17 • Romans 5:7-8
Ephesians 2:4-5 • 1 John 4:9-10

The Bible* calls the story of Jesus, the gospel.* The word gospel means 'good news'. That story begins long before Jesus came to live among us.

God created* all things. He made our first parents, Adam* and Eve.* He made a garden where they could live. God gave then all they needed. They had good work to do. They had each other. They could walk and talk with God. They felt no fear or shame, or guilt.

God gave them all of the fruit from every tree in the garden to eat. But he told them not to eat from one tree. If they ate from that tree, they would die. But Adam and Eve did not obey God. They ate from the tree. When they did, many bad things happened. They felt shame. They became afraid. They knew they had done wrong.

GOD CHOSE TO SHOW MERCY. GOD CHOSE TO GIVE GRACE.

But God did not abandon Adam and Eve. He came back into the garden. God spoke with them. He made clothes for them to cover them. He had mercy on them.

Because they did not obey God, God put them out of the garden. Now they could not know God as they once did. And they and their children went further and further away from God. They did not honor* him as God. They did not thank him for all he had made. They began to worship* the things God had made and not the God who made them. They made idols* and worshipped the gods they created.

Because of this, all people became the enemies of God. They did not honor him. If nothing changed, they would be judged by God.[1] They would die. God would pour out his wrath on them forever.

And they could not make themselves right with God again. Unless God did something for them that they could not do for themselves, they would die for their sins* against God. They deserved God's wrath.*

So, all people, including you, have sinned against God. If God had chosen to do so, he could have done nothing. God did not need to save people. God could have let us go on doing evil* things. He could have let us die and be judged. He could have punished us all.

But God did something for us that we could not do for ourselves. He sent his son to rescue us. Why would God do this? He did this because he loved us. He is a God of mercy and grace.

Mercy is when someone does not punish us when we deserve it. We deserved to face God's anger. We deserved to be punished because we did not honor God. God punished Jesus in our place. God showed us mercy.

But he is not only a God of mercy. He is also a God of grace. Grace is when I receive a good thing when I should get something bad. I deserved to be punished. But God forgave me. When I deserved to be cursed, I received a blessing* instead.

And how did God show his mercy to us? God chose to send his son to rescue us.

He did not have to do this. He would have been right to allow us to receive what we deserved. That would have been justice.* Justice is when I receive what I deserve. Because I am a sinner, what I deserve is God's anger. I deserve to be punished.

But the scriptures* tell us that he did something else. God showed his love for us. Here is how. He sent his son into the world. He sent him so we could receive life through him.[2] This is what love is. It is not that we loved God. It is that God loved us. And he sent his son to give his life to pay for our sins.[3]

This is the good news. God chose to show mercy. God chose to give grace. Why would God choose to show mercy? Why would God choose grace instead of judgement?*

God made this choice because that is the kind of God he is. He is a God who loves those he has made. He is a God who shows mercy. He is a God of grace.

> 'He saved us, not because of the good things we have done. But he saved us because he is a God of mercy.'[4]

---

1. Hebrews 9:27
2. Romans 5:8
3. 1 John 4:9-10

4. Psalm 86:5; Ephesians 2:4; Titus 3:5

Was Jesus* Christ* both God and man?

Yes, Jesus was truly God and truly man.

John 1:1-3 • Philippians 2:5-11 • Colossians 2:9
Hebrews 2:14-18

The scriptures* are clear about the answer to this question. The Bible* tells us that Jesus was truly a man. The scriptures also tell us that Jesus was truly God. He is both God and man at the same time. The scriptures tell us that this is true. But the answer is a mystery to us.

The Bible, in the Gospel* of John,* tells us that Jesus is the one who made all things.[1] He is God. He has always been. He will always be. Then John tells us that the one who made all things 'became flesh.'[2] God the creator* came to be a part of the world he created.* He came to live among his own people.[3]

One day, more than 2000 years ago, an angel* spoke to a woman named Mary.* Mary was a virgin.* She had never been with a man.

The angel said this to Mary. 'The Holy Spirit* will come to you. The power of the Most High will cover you. The holy* child you give birth to will be called the Son of God.'[4] This baby she carried was God in the flesh.

This had never happened before. This will never happen again. God would come into the world. He would be born through the body of a woman. God would be born into this world as a baby. His mother would give him the name Jesus. As God, Jesus is not created. But a body was made for him by a miracle* from the Holy Spirit.

When the disciples* first met Jesus, they understood that he was a man. They saw him as a teacher and a prophet.* They heard him speak of where he lived as a boy. As a young boy, he had to grow and learn. They heard how Satan* had tempted* him. They saw him when he was thirsty. He could be tired. He could be hungry. He needed to sleep. He wept when he lost his friend. He ate bread and drank water just as they did. They heard him pray.

As a man, they saw him suffer in all of the ways that men suffer. They watched him die on a cross.*

But they also saw him do things that only God could do. He made water into wine. He fed 5000 people with only a few loaves of bread and fish. He spoke to a storm and it became calm. He removed evil* spirits* from people to make them well. He was able to give life to a young girl who was dead. He would heal those were sick and in pain. They heard him say that he had come down from heaven.* They heard him say that God was his Father. They heard him forgive* sins.* They heard him say many things about the Law* and the Temple.* They saw him after he had come back from death.

After Jesus rose again from death, the disciples understood. Jesus was truly a man. And Jesus was truly God. So, all that God is, Jesus is. All that we are, Jesus became. He was and had always been God. He became a human being in every way that we are. But there is one way that Jesus was not as we are. Jesus was not born in sin. He was pure and never did anything that did not please God the Father. There was no sin in him.

All that God is,

JESUS IS.

All that we are,

JESUS BECAME.

Jesus is both God[5] and man.[6] It is important that we believe this, even if it is a mystery to us. If we deny that either of these things is true, we will not be right with God. Paul* said that a person cannot be right with God unless they confess* that Jesus is God.[7] John wrote that if a person denies that Jesus was truly a man, they cannot be right with God.[8]

This is a hard thing to understand. Even Jesus' disciples did not understand this until Jesus rose from the dead! When they did understand it, they told everyone everywhere they went.

1. John 1:1–3
2. John 1:14
3. John 1:10–12

4. Luke 2:35
5. John 20:28; Titus 2:13; Hebrews 1:8

6. Romans 1:2–4; 1 John 4:2–3
7. Romans 10:9
8. 2 John 1:7

question —— 067

What work did Jesus* the Savior* do?

He obeyed God in every way, and he took the punishment for sinful* people.

Romans 8:3-4 • Philippians 2:7-8 • Hebrews 4:15
Hebrews 9:14-15

question —— 068

Why did Jesus die?

Jesus put away God's anger by dying in the place of sinful people.

Mark 10:45 • 2 Corinthians 5:19-21 • Galatians 3:13

When Adam* sinned,* our world became a broken place. We became a broken people. We began to do bad things. People began to hurt one another. They began to create their own gods. They did not care for the world as God told them to. The Bible* calls these bad things, sin.

Because God is holy* and good, he does not allow sin. He must punish sinners* when they do evil.* God cannot ignore the wrong things people do. He is a God of justice.*¹ Justice is when we receive from God what we deserve.

That is a big problem for us. It is a big problem because we sin. When we break God's law,* we must pay the price for our failure. We are not right with God. We do not obey God in every way. And because of our sin, we deserve to be punished. We deserve to die. When we broke God's law, we deserved God's angry judgement.*² We deserve to be put away from God forever.

So, how can we be right with God again? How can we escape God's judgement for our sins? By ourselves, we cannot.³ God must do something for us that we cannot do for ourselves. And God did do something. He made a way to solve our problem. God decided to rescue us. So, God the Father sent his Son into the world to do that. He sent Jesus to be the one who saves sinners.⁴

How did Jesus do this?

Jesus lived a life that pleased God in every way. He did something that no one else has ever done. Jesus never sinned. He always told the truth. He always did all that God wanted people to do. Jesus did all that God's law demanded. He lived his life in a way that always pleased God.

Because Jesus was without sin, he did not deserve to die. We were the guilty ones. He was not guilty. But God loved us. And this is how he showed his love. While we were still sinners, God sent Jesus to rescue us.⁵ He loved us so much that, even when we were still sinners, Jesus died for us.

Jesus became a man to sacrifice* himself so that we could live. He would give up his life so that we would not have to die. Jesus would take the guilt* and sin of other people upon himself.[6] He would pay the price that our sin deserved.

Jesus went to the cross.* On the cross, God let his anger for sin fall upon Jesus. And there, on the cross, Jesus died. God poured out all of his wrath* against sin on Jesus. Jesus took the punishment for sinners. He died in our place.

But Jesus did not stay in the grave. God was pleased with the sacrifice* that Jesus made. So, God brought him to life again. Now, because of Jesus, God can forgive* us for all of the bad things we have done.

There is a way for sinners to be right with God. We do not need to die and be put away from God forever. Jesus went to the cross for us. Jesus has died in our place. Jesus has done all that needed to be done to rescue us from God's anger. And Jesus is the only one who can make us right with God. The scriptures* say it this way.

'There is one God. There is one man who can bring people back to God. That man is Jesus Christ.'[7]

All that God demands of us is that we trust him. We believe on his son, Jesus. We bow to Jesus as our Lord* and King. We give up our own way to follow him.

This is how the scriptures tell this story.

'Christ also suffered once for sins. The one who did what is right suffered for those who do not do right. He suffered to bring you to God. His body was put to death. But the Holy Spirit* brought him to life again.'[8]

1. Psalm 89:14; Colossians 3:25
2. Isaiah 13:11; Hebrews 9:27
3. Romans 3:9–20
4. Galatians 4:4–5; 1 John 4:14
5. Romans 5:8
6. 1 John 3:5
7. 1 Timothy 2:5
8. 1 Peter 3:18

question — 069

How could the eternal* Son of God suffer in the place of sinful* people?

Jesus,* the Son of God, became a man.

John 1:14 • Galatians 4:4-5 • Colossians 2:9

question — 070

How did the Son of God become a man?

He was conceived* by the Holy Spirit* and born of the Virgin* Mary.*

Isaiah 7:14 • Matthew 1:18-21

There are many stories of important births in the Bible.*¹

In the first chapters of Genesis, God made a promise to Abraham.* God promised Abraham that he would become a great nation. This nation would bless* all people. But there was a problem. Abraham did not have a son. Abraham's wife, Sarah,* could not have children. And she was too old to have children. But God kept his promise to Abraham. Sarah had a son. She gave birth to the child God had promised.

There are many stories like this in the Bible. At important times in the history of God's people, God used the birth of a child to bring hope.* The stories of the birth of Moses,* Samson,* and Samuel* are like that. So, God's people learned that the promise of the birth of a child was a sign of hope.

The story of the birth of Jesus is that kind of story. But this is the best of those stories. A woman would give birth to a son. This son would be the one to save his people from their sins.* But his birth would be different than any other. He would be born of a woman who had never been with a man.

But how could a woman have a child without a man? How could a virgin give birth to a son?

Since the beginning, a baby begins to grow inside a woman only after she is joined with a man. A baby needs to have a father and a mother. Mary knew this.² Joseph* knew this.³ But something happened that had never happened before. Mary was a virgin. She had never been with a man. But a baby began to grow inside of Mary's body. This child would be God's son. He would have God as his father.

But God did not join himself to Mary as a man joins himself to a woman. God, the maker of all things, created* life in the body of Mary. The Holy Spirit brought a new life into Mary's womb.*

In every other way, the birth of Jesus was just like the birth of any other baby. His body grew in Mary's womb. Mary gave birth to Jesus in the same way that all mothers give birth. But in one way, Jesus' birth was the only one of its kind. Jesus was born of a virgin.

The promise of the birth of a child was a sign of hope.

The Bible tells us that this was a miracle* from God. The Holy Spirit would cause a baby to grow in Mary's body. So, Jesus was the Son of God. And Jesus was Mary's son as well. The baby that was born of Mary was both God and man at the same time. Everything that is true of the nature of God was true of Jesus.[4] Everything that is true of the nature of a man was true of Jesus as well. All except for one thing. Jesus had no sin.

Through the virgin birth, Jesus came into the world that he made. He became a man and lived among us.[5] But why did Jesus, the son of God, need a body?

God is spirit.* He does not have a body like men. Because God is eternal, God cannot die. So how could God suffer in the place of sinful people? How could God take the punishment for men?

To do this, Jesus, the Son of God, became a man. He took on a body so that he became one of us. He became one of us so that he could suffer in our place.[6] Jesus became a human so that he could suffer and take upon himself the suffering that sinful people deserve.

That is not the only reason Jesus became a man. Jesus also became a man to show us what God is like. He became a man to show us the kind of life that pleases God. He came to win a victory over all of the evil* that worked against those he loves.[7] Jesus would show us how to live and set an example for us to follow.[8]

But Luke* tells us that one of the most important reasons Jesus became a man is this. Jesus became a man so that he could suffer and rise from the dead.[9]

---

1. Exodus 2:1-10; Judges 13:1-25;
   1 Samuel 1:1-20
2. Luke 1:34
3. Matthew 1:18-20

4. Colossians 1:19; Colossians 2:9
5. John 1:14; Romans 1:3
6. Hebrews 2:14-18
7. Hebrews 2:14-15; 1 John 3:8

8. John 13:34, 15:12; 1 Peter 2:21
9. Luke 24:16; Acts 17:3

question —— 071

What kind of life did Jesus* Christ* live on earth?

A simple, honorable,* and humble life.

Matthew 8:20 • Matthew 11:28-30 • Luke 4:18-19
2 Corinthians 8:9 • 2 Corinthians 10:1

question —— 072

Did the Lord* Jesus Christ ever sin?*

No, he was holy* and pure.

John 8:29 • 2 Corinthians 5:21 • Hebrews 7:26
1 Peter 2:21-23

Jesus is the son of God. He was one with God the Father and God the Holy Spirit* before he made all things. But when he came as a man, he came as a servant.

Jesus was the one who came to 'save his people from their sins.' He was the son that God promised to Abraham.* He was the prophet* who would be greater than Moses.* Jesus was the son that God promised to David.* He would rule a kingdom* that would never end. But Jesus did not look like a king. He did not live in a big house.¹ He did not guide a great army.

In many ways, Jesus was a common man. As a boy, he grew up in a carpenter's home. He grew and learned. He honored* his parents. He was meek and humble.² He was kind to people who were sick and broken. Jesus went toward people that most people went away from. He sometimes told people that God sent him to give good news to poor people. He sent him to heal people whose hearts* were sad. God sent him to make the blind to see and help those who were in trouble. The common people were glad to hear this.

From the time he was a boy, Jesus knew that he had come from God. He knew that God was his father. So, he lived his life to please his father in every way.³ Jesus did all that his father wanted him to do. He obeyed the law* that God gave Moses. Jesus brought honor to his father in all that he did. He obeyed his father, even when it meant that he would suffer.

It is in this way that Jesus was different from any other person who ever lived. Jesus pleased God in everything he did. He did all of the things God asked him to do. He loved God the Father with all of his heart and soul* and mind. He never had an evil* thought. He never spoke an evil word. Jesus was without sin.

Sin is doing what we should not do. Sin is not doing what we should do. Sin is when we break God's law. Sin is when we rebel against God.[4] But Jesus never sinned. He never did anything that did not please God.

Every person who has been born after Adam* and Eve* has been born in sin. Everyone who has had a human father and mother has a sin nature.[5] But Jesus had no human father. Jesus was the one and only son of the eternal* God. He was born without sin.

Jesus was holy. The word 'holy' means set apart. When we say that Jesus was holy, we mean that he was one of a kind. He was set apart from sin.[6] Jesus was pure in every way.

Why is this important?

In the Old Testament,* when people did an evil thing, they had to bring an offering to the Temple.* They would take a young animal, often a lamb,* from their flock. This lamb had to be perfect. It could not be sick. It could not be blind or have a bad leg. The lamb could not have anything wrong with it.

The person would take the lamb to the priest* at the Temple. The person had to confess* what they had done. But the priest did not punish the person. Instead, the priest would kill the lamb. He would burn part of the lamb on the altar.* He gave the lamb as a sacrifice.* The lamb would give his life to pay for what the sinful person did.

When John the Baptist* first saw Jesus, he called Jesus 'the lamb of God who takes away the sin of the world.'[7] John knew that Jesus would be like a lamb in the Old Testament. If Jesus was to be a sacrifice for his people, he had to be perfect. If Jesus was a sinner,* he would not be able to help us. He could not take away the sins of other people if he was a sinner too. But Jesus would be a perfect sacrifice[8] because Jesus was without sin.

1. Matthew 8:20
2. Matthew 11:29; Philippians 2:7-8
3. Luke 2:41-52
4. 1 John 3:4; Deuteronomy 9:7; Joshua 1:18
5. Psalm 51:5; Romans 5:12, 17, 19
6. 2 Corinthians 5:21; Hebrews 4:14; 1 Peter 2:2; 1 John 3:5
7. John 1:29; John 1:36
8. 1 Peter 1:18-19; 1 John 3:5

question —— 073

What kind of death did Jesus* Christ* die?

Christ died on a cross.*

Luke 23:33 • Galatians 3:13 • Philippians 2:8

question —— 074

Did Christ remain in the grave after he died?

No, Christ rose from death on the third day.

Matthew 28:5-7 • Luke 24:5-8 • Romans 4:25
1 Corinthians 15:3-4

The Romans* had many ways to punish bad people in Jesus' day. They sometimes beat them. They sometimes put them in prison. For the people who were most evil,* they put them to death. One of the ways they did this was to hang them on a cross until they were dead. That is what they did to Jesus.

The men who wrote the Gospels* tell us the story. First, the leaders of the Jews* arrested Jesus. Then they took him before their leaders. These men wanted to judge Jesus. They wanted to prove that Jesus had broken their laws.* But they could not find that Jesus did anything wrong. So, men came to tell lies about Jesus. They took Jesus to both the Jews and the Roman leaders. No one could find that Jesus did anything wrong. But this did not stop them. They did not like what he had been saying. The leaders were afraid that people would follow Jesus instead of following them. They had already decided that Jesus needed to die.

They decided that they should punish Jesus. So, they whipped Jesus with leather cords. They took rods made of wood and beat him. They made a crown from sharp thorns and put it on Jesus' head. That hurt Jesus very much. They also hit Jesus in the face with their hands. They took his clothes from him to shame him. They spoke cruel, angry words about him. They laughed to see him in pain. Then they made Jesus carry a big cross made of wood. They put nails in his hands and feet to fasten his body to the cross. Then they lifted the cross.

Jesus died. He was buried. He rose to life again.

Jesus hung on the cross for many hours. Many people sat down and watched him as he died. He cried out many times from the cross. But no one helped him. After some time, Jesus died. Then soldiers put a spear through his side to make sure that he was dead. Blood and water came out of his side.

Jesus was dead. He had died on that cross. But it is important to remember what Jesus had told his disciples.* No one had the power to take his life from him.[2] Neither the Jews nor the soldiers took Jesus' life from him. Jesus chose to lay down his life for those he loved.

Later, men took his body down from the cross. They wrapped his body in cloths to be buried. They put his body in a cave and closed the entrance with a huge stone. We call a cave where someone is buried a 'tomb.'* They wanted to bury Jesus before the holy* day. The holy day was the last day of the week.

So, Jesus' body was in the tomb the day before the Sabbath.* He was in the tomb all of the Sabbath. He was in the tomb the day after the Sabbath.

On the morning of the first day of the week, some women went to the tomb. They went there to put oil and spices on the body of Jesus. But when they came to the cave, they saw that Jesus' body was not there. They also saw an angel.* The angel spoke to them. He said, 'He is not here. He has risen.' The women were afraid. But they were also very happy. So they went to tell the men who had followed Jesus, just as the angel had told them. Jesus was no longer dead. He was alive. He had risen from the dead.

That night, Jesus came to see his friends. They all saw him. They ate with him. Many other people saw him too.

'Christ has risen' is an important truth to Christians.[3] For if Jesus was not raised from the dead, no one could hope* that anything Jesus said was true. But since he did rise from the dead, it proved all that he said was true.

God raised Jesus to life. Jesus is truly the Son of God.[4] He had power over death.[5] He did die in the place of sinners,* and his sacrifice* pleased God.[6] Jesus will return from heaven* one day to judge the world.[7] Because Jesus was raised from the dead, all of those who believe in him will also be raised.[8] God showed us that all of these things are true when he raised Jesus from death.

Jesus died. He was buried. He rose to life again. That is good news.[9]

---

1. Matthew 27; Mark 15; Luke 23;
   John 19
2. John 10:17-18
3. Acts 1:3; Acts 2:24-35; Acts 3:15
   Acts 4:10; Acts 5:30-32;
   Acts 13:33-37

4. Romans 1:4; John 20:24-31
5. Acts 2:24; Romans 6:9-10;
   Revelation 1:18
6. Romans 4:24-25; Hebrews 10:12
7. Acts 17:30-31

8. Romans 8:11;
   1 Corinthians 15:22-23;
   2 Corinthians 4:14
9. 1 Corinthians 15:3-4;
   Romans 10:9-10

question — 075

Who will God rescue from the result of their sin?*

God will rescue those who repent* of sin and believe on the Lord* Jesus* Christ.*

Mark 1:14-15 • John 3:16-18 • Acts 20:21

question — 076

What does it mean to repent?

To repent is to be sorry for my sin and to turn from my sin because it offends God.

Luke 19:8-10 • 2 Corinthians 7:9-10
1 Thessalonians 1:9-10

When people hear the good news about Jesus, they must act on it in some way. They will either accept it. Or they will refuse it.

But what do I need to do to accept the good news about Jesus? What must I do to be rescued from the results of my sin?

The Bible* uses two words to answer that question.

I must repent. And I must believe.

Sometimes, the words repent and believe are used together in the Bible. When Jesus told people about his kingdom*, he told them that they must 'repent and believe the good news'¹ to be a part of it. Paul* reminded a group of church* leaders that his message was always the same.

'Repent of your sin and turn to God. And believe on the Lord Jesus.'²

Sometimes, the words repent and believe are found by themselves. When Peter* or John the Baptist* or Paul wanted people to come to Jesus, they told people to repent.³ Jesus even said that if they did not repent, they would die.⁴ But he did not mention the word believe. At other times, both Jesus and Paul told people that they needed to believe to be right with God.⁵ And they did not mention the word repent.

So how do those two words fit together?

The more you read the Bible, the more you understand how the Bible uses these words. Although the terms are sometimes used alone, repent and believe always belong together. They are two parts of the same thing. Just as a coin has two sides, there are two sides to how people must reply to the good news about Jesus. A person cannot truly believe and not repent. Nor can a person truly repent and not believe.

Think of it this way.

Imagine that you are walking to a village. You start down a path that you think will take you there. But after you have gone a long way, you see a sign. The sign says that the way you are going is not the way to the village. You were going away from it.

What would you do?

First, you would decide if you believe that what the sign says is true. And if you believe the sign, you will stop. You will turn and go the other way. When you believed, it meant you would also change your direction.

That is what it means to repent and believe. When you come to hear the good news about Jesus and believe that it is true, you turn away from your old way to go a new way. You will change.

You must first change your mind about who Jesus is. Before you heard the story of Jesus, maybe you did not know about him at all. Or maybe you believed that he was only a wise man. Or maybe you thought he was only a man in a story that someone made up. But now you come to understand that Jesus is God. You understand that he came as a man to live among us. And that Jesus will forgive* you and rescue you if you go to him.

When you change how you think about Jesus, that leads to other changes. Before you came to believe in Jesus, you may have done bad things. And when you did these things, you did not care. You did not feel bad about doing them. But now you see that God hates sin. Now you know that God is not pleased when you do those things. So, you feel regret when you act badly. You have changed your mind about sin.

The prophets* in the Old Testament* often called on the people to repent. Many times, the people turned away from the true God to worship* false gods. They followed the false gods of the nations about them. When they did this, the prophets called them to turn away from the false gods and turn back to God. It is always that way.

The word 'repent' means a change of mind. But it goes far beyond that. When you repent, you see sin for what it is. You see Jesus for who he is. And you turn away from one to turn to follow the other. You cannot turn to Jesus without turning away from sin.

———

JESUS WILL FORGIVE YOU AND RESCUE YOU IF YOU GO TO HIM.

———

1. Mark 1:14-15
2. Acts 20:21

3. Matthew 3:1-12; Acts 2:38;
   Acts 17:30

4. Luke 13:1- 5
5. Acts 16:31

What does it mean to believe or to have faith* in Christ?

To have faith in Christ* is to believe in Jesus.* We trust* only in him to save* us.

John 14:6 • Acts 4:12 • 1 Timothy 2:5 • 1 John 5:11-12

How does a sinner* come to meet the Savior?* They believe in the one who raised Jesus our Lord* from the dead.[1] God rescues those who believe.

The Bible* says this in many ways. Peter* and Paul* say that we are made right with God through faith.[2] We are put right with God when we believe in the Lord Jesus Christ.[3] The Psalms* tell us that God saves those who put their trust in him.[4] All of these words – faith, trust, and believe, are different ways of saying the same thing. And each word helps us to understand the other words.

Luke* tells us a story that will help us understand this. Jesus was eating at a man's home. A woman came into the house as they were eating. She had not been invited to the meal. But she came over to Jesus. She began to cry, and her tears fell on Jesus' feet. The woman wiped the tears from his feet with her hair. Then she put valuable oil on his feet. She did all of this to show her love for Jesus. But the other people at the meal were not happy. They knew that this woman had done many bad things. But Jesus did not speak badly about her. Instead, he turned to her and said,

'Your sins* are forgiven.* Go in peace.* Your faith has saved you.'[5]

The woman had come to know who Jesus was. She trusted that he was kind. She had come to believe that he would welcome her if she went to him. So, that is what she did. She honored* him. She trusted that he would show her mercy.* And she acted in a way that showed her faith.

---

1. Romans 4:25
2. Romans 5:1–5; 1 Peter 1:5
3. Acts 16:31

4. Psalm 13:5; Psalm 22:4–5;
   Psalm 62:8; Psalm 86:2;
   Psalm 91:14

5. Luke 7:36–50

Can you repent* and believe in Christ* by your own power?

No, I must have the help of the Holy Spirit.*

Jeremiah 13:23 • John 3:5-6 • John 6:44
1 Corinthians 2:14

Before I came to Jesus*, I was bound up in my sin* and blind to the truth.¹ I was not looking for God.² I did not know God. And I did not want to know him. The good news about Jesus did not sound like good news to me. I could not respond to God. It was like I was dead to God and God was dead to me. I had no way to react to God because my spirit* was dead. I could not help myself. All of these problems needed to be solved or I could never have believed.

One of the prophets* named Jeremiah* said it this way:

'You are in the habit of doing evil.* Do you think you can change your ways? You have as much chance of that as a leopard has of changing his spots.'

Paul* said the same kind of thing in a letter many years later.

'Some people do not have the Holy Spirit,' he said. 'So, they do not accept the things that come from the Spirit of God. Those things are foolish to them. They cannot understand them.'³

So how do I explain how I have gone from not believing to believing in Jesus? How did I go from going away from God to being a follower* of Jesus?

The answer is:
the work of the Holy Spirit.

God the Holy Spirit is one with God the Father and Jesus, God's Son. All of the persons, Father, Son and Spirit, are the one true God. It is God who, by grace,* has made salvation* possible.[4] God the Father planned a way to rescue sinful* people. Jesus, the Son of God, did all that needed to be done to complete this plan. He lived a perfect life. He died on the cross.* God raised him from the dead. God the Holy Spirit applies the work that Jesus did to people's hearts.* Paul says that no person can say Jesus is Lord* except by the Holy Spirit.[5]

The Holy Spirit made sure that I heard the gospel.* Then he made me able to understand that the story of Jesus is true. He helped me see that my sin did not please God. I saw that I would be judged by God for the bad things that I had done.[6] The Holy Spirit gave me a desire to find out how I could be changed. The Holy Spirit gave me eyes to see.

I must make a decision. I must choose to confess* that Jesus Christ is Lord. But I am not able to say that without a work of the Holy Spirit. The Holy Spirit freed me from being a slave to my sin to being free to choose and follow Jesus. I went from being dead in my sins to being alive in Jesus because the Spirit gave me life.[7] Every step in the journey from being an enemy of God to being received into God's family is a gift from God.

When we believe in Jesus, many things in our lives change. God forgives us for all the bad things we have done. God welcomes us into his family. The Holy Spirit works in us to make us more like Jesus. He leads us and comforts us and helps us know when we need to repent and turn back to God.[8]

The Prophet Jonah* found himself inside a fish. There he prayed to God for help. He said in his prayer,

'God is the one who saves.'[9]

If I am a Christian, I must never forget to thank the Holy Spirit.

---

1. 2 Corinthians 4:3-4
2. Romans 3:10-18
3. 1 Corinthians 2:14

4. Ephesians 2:1-10
5. John 6:44
6. John 16:8-9

7. John 3:6-8; John 6:63
8. 2 Timothy 2:24-26
9. Jonah 2:9

question ——

079

Where do people hear the truth about Christ?*

In the gospel,* the good news that offers a Savior* to all people.

Mark 1:1 • Acts 15:7 • Romans 1:16-17

The word, gospel, means the good message or good news. People used the word long before Jesus* came. When people were at war, they would wait to hear word of how the battle was going. When a messenger came to say their soldiers had won, he carried the good news. The prophet* Isaiah* talked about this. He said, 'How beautiful are the feet of him who brings good news.'[1]

Sometimes, when a new king took his place to rule the people, he sent messengers to tell the 'good news.'

In the New Testament,* the word, 'gospel,' also means good news. John the Baptist* and Jesus brought good news about the kingdom* of God. The good news was that the king, the Messiah,* had come. The kingdom of heaven* was near.[2]

When Paul* and the apostles* write their letters, they used the word gospel to tell the good news about Jesus. They told about who Jesus is and what he had done. They called this message the gospel of Jesus Christ. But the gospel is also about how the work of Jesus affects people.

Gospel means the good message.

We can only see the gospel as good news when we understand the bad news. The bad news is that we are all sinners.* We have not shown honor* to God. We have not followed his laws.* Because God is holy,* people who do bad things cannot be in God's presence. And we are not able to do enough good things to make things right with God. Only God can make a way for sinful* people to be right with him. The gospel is about what God did for sinful people. Christ died 'for us.'

Jesus took the punishment that we deserved. He paid for our sin with his life. He gave his life in death so that we could live.

Because of what Jesus did, I can be forgiven* for my sins. The good news is that, when I believe in Jesus, I am no longer an enemy of God. I have become a part of God's family. This is why the gospel is so important. It is the message God uses to rescue people from their sin.* Paul said that the gospel brings salvation.*[3]

People hear the message about Jesus. Then they see that the message is true.[4] When they obey[5] the call of the gospel to believe, they are saved.[6] God rescues them from their sin and gives them hope.*[7]

Sometimes people use the word gospel to talk about the first four books of the New Testament. So, we call the books of Matthew,* Mark,* Luke* and John* – The Gospels. Sometimes, the word is used of all that Jesus said and did. That is the way that Mark uses it. But, most often, the Bible* uses the word in one way. The gospel is the message about who Jesus is and what he has done.

Paul wrote a letter to the church* in a city named Corinth.* Some of the people did not remember what Paul had said about the gospel. So, he wrote to remind them.

'I want to remind you of the gospel I told you about. It is the news that you received and believed. It is what I received and passed on to you. Christ died for our sins, just as the scripture* said he would. He was buried. He was raised on the third day, just as the scriptures said he would.'[8]

This good news is a most important thing. Jesus is alive. He is the Messiah king. He has won the victory over evil* and death. And God will rescue all who trust* him.

Jesus told his followers* to go all over the world to tell people the gospel.[9] The gospel is the message God will use to rescue all who believe it is true. If people do not hear the gospel, they will never believe. If they do not believe, they will not be saved.[10]

Jesus said that all of the Old Testament* scriptures speak about him. And the Holy Spirit* helped the apostles record the gospel for us in the New Testament. So, the entire Bible tells the story of the good news about Jesus.

---

1. Isaiah 52:7; Romans 10:15
2. Mark 1:15; Matthew 3:2;
   Matthew 4:17; Luke 4:43
3. Romans 1:16; Ephesians 1:13;
   Titus 2:11-12
4. Galatians 2:5,14; Colossians 1:15
5. 1 Peter 4:17; Romans 1:5;
   2 Thessalonians 1:8
6. John 3:15-16; Acts 16:31;
   Romans 10:9; 1 Corinthians 1:21
7. Colossians 1:23
8. 1 Corinthians 15:1-4
9. Matthew 28:16-20
10. Romans 10:14-15

question ——
080

What now has Jesus* our Savior* become to us?

Jesus Christ* has become our Prophet,* our Priest* and our King.

Matthew 13:57 • John 18:37 • Hebrews 1:1-3
Hebrews 5:5-6 • Revelation 1:5

question ——
081

How is Jesus Christ a Prophet?

He shows us who God is. And teaches us how to please him.

Deuteronomy 18:18 • John 1:18 • John 4:25-26
Acts 3:22 • 1 John 5:20

question ——
082

Why do we need Christ as a Prophet?

Because we cannot know God without him.

Matthew 11:25-27 • John 17:25-26
1 Corinthians 2:14-16

In the Old Testament,* there were three kinds of people who God set apart to do special work for him. In some way, they would act for God. These were prophets, priests, and kings.

The prophets were men and women who spoke for God. God would give a message to the prophets. The prophets would speak that message to the people.

The priests were the men who cared for the temple* where God was present. God chose the priests to go between God and the people to bring them together. They would make the sacrifices* for the people. They did their work so that sins* could be forgiven.*

God chose the kings to rule the people. The king was to lead the nation under God's authority. He was to lead God's people in a way that would honor* God and bless* other nations.

Each of these people were important. In the Old Testament, this was the way God led his people. Jesus the Messiah* came, to do all that the prophets, the priests and the kings before him were to do.

The prophets in the Old Testament spoke for God. There were times when God spoke to people himself. But most of the time, he spoke to the people through the prophets. He gave them authority and the words to speak for him. Most of the prophets had messages for God's people in Israel.* But all of the prophets knew that all of the nations were in God's plans. So, they would sometimes speak messages to the other nations close to them.

When a true prophet spoke, what he said would always happen. His words were just as if God had spoken. The people knew that the word of the true prophet was the word of God. Many of the prophets did signs and wonders. God gave them the power to do miracles* so that people would know that they spoke for him. The prophets were one of the ways God revealed* himself to people.

When Jesus came, he served as the perfect prophet. Jesus was God himself, speaking to people. The voice of God used to come through the prophets. Now, the voice of Jesus is the voice of God. The words of Jesus are the words of God. God revealed himself in all that Jesus was and did and said. The writer of the book of Hebrews says it this way.

> 'In the past God spoke to our people through the prophets. He spoke to them many times. And he spoke in many different ways. Now in these last days, God has spoken to us through his Son.'[1]

When he first began to do his work, Jesus read from the prophet Isaiah.*

> 'The Spirit* of the Lord* God is on me, because the Lord has chosen me to bring good news to poor people. He has sent me to heal those with a sad heart.* He has sent me to tell those in prison that they can go free.'[2]

After he read Isaiah's words, he said. 'The scripture* you have just heard has come true this very day.'[3] Jesus told his disciples* that everything that he said was what God his Father had told him to say.[4] Before he went to the cross,* he prayed. In that prayer to the Father he said, 'I gave them the words you gave to me.'[5] Jesus understood that he was speaking for God, just as the prophets had.

Jesus would not only tell who God is and what he is like. Jesus would show what God is like by his life. He would say, 'If you have seen me, you have seen the Father.'[6] And just as with all true prophets, what Jesus said would happen did happen. He told his disciples that he would be put to death long before it happened. He said that he would be raised from death. He knew that Judas* would betray him and that Peter* would deny him. He knew that his disciples would leave him before each of these things happened. This was the sign of a true prophet.

Jesus also did many miracles. God had done these same kinds of things through the prophets like Moses,* Elijah,* and Elisha.* These miracles were signs that Jesus truly spoke for God.

When people heard Jesus and saw what he did, they knew Jesus was a prophet. They spoke of him as a prophet. And Jesus agreed with them when they said that he was a prophet. He even used the title to speak about himself.[7] Jesus' role as prophet did not end when he went back into the heavens. Jesus' ministry* as a prophet continues today through the Holy Spirit.* Jesus gathered his apostles* as they ate the Passover* meal together. He told them that he would send the Holy Spirit to them. The Holy Spirit 'will cause you to remember everything that I have said to you,' he said.[8] Later, the Holy Spirit would guide them to write down what they remembered. There, in the written words, Jesus, our perfect prophet, still speaks. He would make sure that the words they wrote were the words of God. The New Testament* would be the message from God the Father, through Christ the Word, given by the Holy Spirit.

1. Hebrews 1:1-2
2. Luke 4:18; and see Isaiah 61:1-2
3. Mark 4:16-21
4. John 7:16; John 8:28
5. John 17:8
6. John 14:9; and see John 1:18
7. Matthew 16:14; Matthew 21:11; Luke 7:16; John 1:23; John 4:19; John 9:17; and see Matthew 13:57; Mark 6:4; Luke 4:24; Luke 13:13; John 4:44
8. John 14:26

083

How is Jesus* Christ* a Priest?*

He died in our place and speaks to God for us.

Psalm 110:4 • Hebrews 4:14-16 • Hebrews 7:24-25
1 John 2:1-2

084

Why do we need Christ as a Priest?

Because our sin* has made us guilty and ashamed.

Proverbs 20:9 • Ecclesiastes 7:20 • Isaiah 53:6
Romans 3:10-12 • Romans 3:23 • James 2:10

Priests were the people who cared for the temple.* Priests led the times of worship* for the people of Israel.* But the priest's most important task was to make offerings* or offer sacrifices* to God for the people.[1] They stood between God and the people to connect them. When someone sinned, the law* of Moses* said they had to bring a sacrifice. This sacrifice would be a sign that the people were sorry for the bad thing they had done. It was also a way to avoid the punishment that they deserved. They would bring an animal to the priests. The priest would kill the animal. He would take parts of the animal and burn them with fire on the altar.* Some of the blood would be poured out on the ground or put on the sides of the altar. The animal, who had done nothing wrong, would die in the place of the one who had sinned.

Why were the priests so important? Only the priest could make a sacrifice. No one could come to God on their own. Only the priests could go into the temple to do acts of worship there. And only one special priest, the High Priest, could go into the Most Holy* place. The Most Holy place was where God was present in a special way. The High Priest would make a special sacrifice. This offering was to cover the sins of the whole nation. He would go into this Most Holy place once a year and offer the blood from the sacrifice to God.

The writer of the book of Hebrews knew a lot about the work of the priests in the temple. So he uses many of the words that speak of priests and sacrifices in the temple to speak about Jesus. He calls Jesus our Great High Priest.[2]

Here is what Hebrews says about Jesus.

In the Old Testament,* the priests had to make the same sacrifices over and over. The High Priest would go into the Most Holy Place, and the next year he would have to go again. But when Jesus died, he died as a sacrifice. He made this sacrifice once, and it would never need to be made again.[3] In the Old Testament, when the High Priest died, another priest would take his place. But Jesus is alive and lives forever. So, he will be our priest forever. Under the law of Moses, priests would need to make a sacrifice for their own sin before they could go into the Most Holy Place.

But Jesus did not need to be forgiven.* Jesus obeyed God in every way. He had no sin. Because he was perfect, he could offer a perfect sacrifice. And Jesus himself was that sacrifice. On the cross,* Jesus was the Lamb* of God. By his death, he would take away sin. But the work of Jesus as our priest did not end on the cross. Jesus rose from the grave and now sits with God the Father. There, as our High Priest, Jesus prays for us. Jesus, the Son whom God loves, speaks to the Father for us as our friend. Jesus knows how to speak to God for us because Jesus became one of us. He can understand our weakness. He knew what it was like to be tempted.* But he did not sin. This is why we can go to God and not be afraid. So, we know that we will find mercy* when we come to pray. Because Jesus is our High Priest, we know that God will give us grace* to help us in our time of need.[4]

One more important part of being a priest was the job of seeing that the people were free from sickness. If they had a skin sickness, the priest had to say that they were not clean. That meant that the sick person could not worship at the temple. They had to live outside of the community.* When someone came near them, they had to say 'Unclean! Unclean!' This was to warn people not to come close. In that time, people thought this sickness was a curse* from God. People with this sickness were called 'lepers.'* These men and women lived with great shame because of this. The people during the time of Moses and of Jesus had no cure for this sickness. People believed that only God could make the leper better. When a leper

> **Jesus rose from the grave and now sits with God the Father.**

saw that his sickness was gone, he, first, had to present himself to the priest. The priest would make sure he was well. Then he would make a sacrifice for the leper. And the leper was declared by the priest to be clean. He could go back to his family. He could come to the temple again. He was welcomed into his community again. His shame had been removed.[5]

Jesus healed many lepers during his life.[6] The Bible* uses words that mean 'to wash' and 'to clean' to talk about how Jesus removes our sin. Because of his sacrifice for us, he makes us clean.[7] He takes away our shame. He made a way for us to be welcomed into the presence of God. He is our High Priest.

————

WE KNOW THAT WE WILL FIND MERCY WHEN WE COME TO PRAY BECAUSE JESUS IS OUR HIGH PRIEST.

————

1. Leviticus 16
2. Hebrews 4:14
3. Hebrews 7:27
4. Hebrews 10:19-23

5. Leviticus 13-14
6. Matthew 8:1-3; Matthew 11:5; Luke 17:11-19

7. 1 Corinthians 6:11; Titus 3:5; Hebrews 9:13-14; 1 John 1:7; 1 John 1:9; Revelation 7:14

question —— 085

How is Jesus* Christ* a King?

He rules over us and defends us.

Psalm 2:6-9 • Ephesians 1:19-23 • Revelation 15:3-4

question —— 086

Why do we need Christ as a King?

Because we are weak and afraid.

2 Corinthians 12:9-10 • Philippians 4:13
Colossians 1:11-13 • Hebrews 13:5-6 • 2 Timothy 1:12

When the Bible* spoke of the Messiah,* it said that the Messiah would be many things to God's people. The Messiah would speak for God as a prophet.* The Messiah would also serve as a priest.* He would represent men before God. And by the sacrifice* he made, he would take away the sin* of his people once and for all.

There was also a third role that the Messiah would fill. He would be born a King.[1]

Long ago, God had made a promise to David.* He said, 'Your house and your kingdom* will last forever.' So, the Jews* waited for this king who they began to call the Messiah. They gave him the name, the 'Son of David.' The angel* Gabriel* told Mary* that her son Jesus would be the one whom God would send to be that King. 'He will be great and will be called the son of the Most High. The Lord* will give him the throne* of his father David.'[2]

Gabriel said that Jesus would come from the family of David. As the son of David, Jesus would rule the people as David did. The people knew that as long as David was king all would be well. David was good. His decisions were fair and right for all his people.[3] And David was strong. No enemy could defeat them as long as David was king.

The Jews thought that the Messiah would be a king like the ones they had had before. He would lead an army and defeat their enemies. But Jesus did not come this way. He came to defeat something stronger than their enemies. He came to put away sin and death.[4]

Jesus is not just the King of the Jews. He is not only King of the nations. Jesus is King over all that he has made. Even the winds and the waves obey him.[5] Jesus also rules as King in the hearts* of his people. He opens their hearts. Jesus rules in such a way so that sin cannot rule over them any longer.[6] His grace* rules in their hearts. And because they love Jesus, they keep his commands.

After Jesus rose from the dead, he went back to be with the father in heaven.* The Book of Revelation* says that, now, Jesus stands at the throne of God. As King, Jesus has control of all things. Jesus' Kingdom will never end.[7] And as King, Jesus will be the judge of all people.[8] He has all authority in heaven and on earth. It is by this authority that he is able to give eternal* life to those the Father has given him.

Jesus is the King of kings and the Lord of lords.[9] This name shows that he is more powerful than any king who has ever lived or who will ever come. There is no power, no king, and no lord who could ever oppose him and win.

In the last days, Jesus will prove to be the one who crushes Satan,* the Evil One.* Jesus won over Satan at the cross* and when he came back from death. When he died and rose from death, he took away the power of death. He made it impossible for the Evil One to win.[10]

Today, Jesus is King. Those of us who follow Jesus do not need to fear. He is good. All he does is right and just. He is strong. Nothing can separate us from his love. He will protect what we have put into his care.[11]

JESUS IS THE KING OF KINGS AND THE LORD OF LORDS.

But Jesus will show that he is King most clearly when he returns. All people will see him in his glory.*[12] He will bring all of his people up from the grave. He will make everything new that was broken. He will make a new heaven and a new earth. From this new place, he will sit on his throne as King.[13]

1. Matthew 2:2
2. Luke 1:32–33
3. 2 Samuel 8:15
4. 1 Corinthians 15:54–57
5. Mark 4:41
6. Romans 6:7–14

7. Matthew 1:1; Revelation 22:16; compare Luke 1:32–33
8. Compare Luke 1:32; Daniel 7:27; Matthew 25:31–46; Daniel 7:13–14
9. Revelation 17:14; Revelation 19:16

10. Compare Colossians 2:15; 1 Corinthians 15:54–57
11. 2 Timothy 1:12
12. Matthew 24:30; Matthew 25:3; Revelation 1:7
13. Revelation 22:1

question ——

087

What blessings* do we receive when we believe* in Jesus* Christ?*

God forgives* us and declares us to be righteous.* God receives us into his family as his own dear children. God makes us holy* in heart* and in behavior. God makes us perfect in body and soul* at the resurrection.*

Romans 5:18 • Galatians 4:4-6 • Ephesians 1:5
Hebrews 10:10-14 • 1 John 3:2

When God saves a person, he blesses* them in many ways. The first way God blesses us is when he says that we are right with God.

If a person breaks a law,* they must stand before a judge. When the judge hears what they have done, he says that the person is guilty and punishes them. This is right and just. One day, all people will stand before God to be judged. He knows all that people have done. He knows every thought and word. So, he is the perfect judge. But this is a problem. God is holy, pure, and perfect. But we are not. We have not honored* him or lived in a way that pleases him. So how can God accept sinful* people? We need to be forgiven.

God sent Jesus to rescue us from the judgement* we deserve. He came to our world as a man. He did all that God asked. He honored God in every way. Then, Jesus died on the cross.* He took our place. God put our sin on Jesus.[1] Then he rose from death and went back to be with God the Father. Now, God looks at what Jesus has done, and he covers the record of our sins with all of the good that Jesus did. God accepts the death of Jesus in our place. He puts the good work of Jesus on our record. Now, he sees us as right and good. He says of us,

'Because of what Jesus has done for you, you are right with God.'[2]

God not only forgives us when we ask. God welcomes us into his family as his dear children.[3]

QUESTION 87 | 179

To adopt* someone is to take a person who is not in your family and make them a legal son or daughter. God adopts sinful people because he is a God of grace.* A child who was adopted in the Roman* family received a new life, a new home, a new father. When God welcomes us into his family, we receive these things too. God makes us one of his family. Jesus is our Lord.* He is the one who saves us. And now, Jesus welcomes us as his brother or sister. We now can come to God and call him our Father.

God did not require us to be like Jesus to receive these blessings. God says that we are right with him as soon as we believe.[4] But his work in us is only beginning. He gives us his Holy Spirit* so we can know that we are his. The Holy Spirit in us is a sign that we belong to God's family.

God gives us his Spirit* and begins to make us more and more like Jesus. The Holy Spirit changes our sinful desires into a desire to please God in every way. He helps us to say no to sin. He shapes our hearts so that we love what God loves and hate what God hates. And he helps us to love all people the way that God loves them. He helps us to forgive those who have done bad things to us. He works in us so that we will be filled with love, joy, and peace.* He helps us to be gentle, and he makes us wise so that we know how to care for other people. He gives us the power to do all that he asks us to do.

But God's work in us will not be complete until Jesus comes again. Jesus will come again in the last days. Then, he will make everything new that was broken. He will give a new body to all of those who have trusted him. That body will never be sick and will never die. He will remove from us all desire to sin and do wrong. Then we will be just like God's son, Jesus, in our hearts and in our behavior.[5]

That is the believer's great hope* for the future. God will make all things right and keep it that way forever.

When we put our faith* and hope in Jesus, God saves us. He blesses us with 'salvation.'* This means that God declares that we are now right with him. He welcomes us into his family as his own dear children. His Holy Spirit is working to remove everything in us that does not please God. He is at

GOD MAKES US ONE OF HIS FAMILY.

work to make us like Jesus. And we look forward to a day when we will be rescued from our sin fully and completely. We will never have to say we are sorry again. We will never feel guilt or shame. We will know how it feels to please God in every way.

1. Romans 5:18-19;   3. Galatians 4:3-7   5. Romans 8:18;
   2 Corinthians 5:21   4. John 1:12   1 Corinthians 15:51-53; 1 John 3:2
2. Romans 5:1

088

Does God give me these blessings* because I have earned them by my good behavior?

No, God gives me these blessings because of his grace.* I do not deserve them and I cannot earn them.

Isaiah 64:6 • Ephesians 2:8-9 • Titus 3:4-7

God does not bless* people because they have earned it.

All people from the first man until now, are sinners.* Our sin* has ruined every part of who we are. Our mind is affected by sin. So, we do not have thoughts that please God. Our desires have been hurt by sin. We follow our own wants and only want to please ourselves. We do not care what God wants. We use our bodies in ways that do not honor* God. We have sinned against the one who made us. God is holy* and his eyes are too pure to approve evil*.[1] The good things we do are like dirty rags to God.[2] We all fall short and do not honor God.[3] What we deserve is death.[4]

But we believe that we are not so bad. And many people believe that if they do enough good things God will reward them. They think they can earn a good standing with God by hard work. And then, God will owe them a reward. He must forgive* them. He must give them life and take them to heaven.*

Many people in the world believe this is true. So, they follow the paths of other gods or spirits. Some people believe that if they do not hurt other people and follow the good path, they will reach a place of peace.* This may take many lifetimes. But they believe that if they do enough good, they can reach perfect happiness.

Other people follow another way. They believe that if they follow the ways of their holy book, that God may reward their good work. They must say the correct prayers, eat the correct foods, and honor holy days and places. They must remove the sin inside themselves. When they do these things, their god may welcome them into heaven.

But the Bible* tells us that God does not save people because of the good things they have done. God saves people by grace. Grace is a word that speaks of the blessing or kindness of God. What do we mean when we say that God saves us by grace? We mean that

God chose to bless us rather than curse* us as our sins deserve. The blessings that God gives come to us as a gift.

If a man works for a reward, his pay is not a gift. It is something he has earned. But God does not save a person because they have worked to earn it. God rescues people from the punishment of their sins because they have put their trust* in Jesus.*

When God rescues us, he forgives our sins. He gives us his Holy Spirit.* He gives us new life. And one day, he will welcome us into his new heaven and new earth.

None of these blessings are things we get by our good works. They come to us by grace. We deserve to be punished for the bad things we do. But God does not punish us. He shows us mercy.* Mercy means that God does not punish us as we deserve to be punished. But, more than this, he blesses us instead. This is grace.

God saves people because he is a God of grace. His salvation* is a gift that we do not deserve, and we cannot earn. He gives this grace to those who put their trust in his son, Jesus.[5]

> **When God rescues us, he forgives our sins. He gives us his Holy Spirit. He gives us new life.**

God shows his love for us in that while we were still sinners, Christ* died for us.[6] If you are a Christian, it is because of God's grace.

---

1. Habakkuk 1:13
2. Isaiah 64:6
3. Romans 3:23
4. Romans 6:23

5. Romans 3:28; Romans 4:4-5; Romans 5:1; Galatians 2:16; Ephesians 1:13; Ephesians 2:8; Philippians 3:9

6. Romans 5:8

question —— 089

Will God ever remove His blessings* from those who truly repent* and believe?

No, Jesus* will never leave those who trust* him to save* them.

John 10:27-30 • Romans 8:38-39 • Philippians 1:6
1 Peter 1:3-5

question —— 090

What is the grace* of God?

The grace of God is his love and goodness to us when we do not deserve it.

Luke 19:8-10 • 2 Corinthians 7:9-10
1 Thessalonians 1:9-10

When we come to God, he shows us both grace and mercy.* The two words are alike in some ways. But they are not quite the same. When we speak of God's mercy, we are saying that God holds back the punishment that we deserve. God cancels the punishment for our sins.* He did this when he made Jesus a sacrifice* for our sin and when Jesus died in our place.[1]

When we speak of God's grace, we are saying that God gives us blessings that we do not deserve. He forgives our sin.[2] He gives us the Holy Spirit.* He blesses* us with every blessing in Christ.[3]

But can we lose these gifts that God has given us? Will God ever take them away from us?

There may be many reasons that we put our hope* in Jesus. But one of those reasons was that we trusted that God could and would keep his promises to us. When he said he would give us eternal* life, we believed that he would do that. When he said that we would never perish, we believed him. When he said that we would not face God's anger and judgement,* we believed that he was telling us the truth.[4] We believed that God could be trusted to keep his promises. When we submit* ourselves to his care, we believed that he could protect what we put in his care.[5]

God chose to adopt* us and welcome us into his family. He promises us that, as his children, we will receive all that he has waiting for us.

In the days of Jesus, a Roman* father could say to a son born in his family that he was not part of the family any longer. He would not receive all that belonged to the father when the father died. But a Roman father could not do this to a son that he had adopted. Roman law would not allow this. The adopted son would be certain to receive all that belonged to his new father.

The people who read Paul's* letter knew this. Paul told them, that when they believe, God adopts them into his family. And that meant they could never lose their place in the family.

God loves his children. Nothing can separate us from the love of God.[6] When we heard the good news about Jesus and believed, God gave us eternal life. We put ourselves in his care. Because Jesus is the son of God, no one can take us away from him. And because Jesus and his Father are one, no one can steal us away from God's care.[7]

When we trust Jesus, we become God's own sons and daughters. And he brings us into his family for a purpose. His purpose for us is that we become just like his son, Jesus.[8] He wants us to be like Jesus in our heart* and in our behavior. That is the work that the Holy Spirit does in us. He breaks the power of sin in us. He gives us a new heart and a new desire to be holy.*[9] God keeps those who have put their faith* in Jesus forever. He does this because of his grace. And he is able to do this by his own power.

It is God who saves us. We do not and cannot save ourselves. God began his work in us when he opened our eyes to see the truth of the gospel.* By his Holy Spirit, he worked in us a desire to know Jesus. The Holy Spirit prepared our hearts to be open to the good news about Jesus. He helped us to see that the gospel was true. And we believed that Jesus is the one who could save us. Then we called on him as Lord.* That is the good work that God began in us.

But this was only the beginning of God's work in us. When we believe in Jesus, the Holy Spirit comes to live in us. He is present in us and always with us. The Holy Spirit in us is a sign that we belong to God. And the Holy Spirit is God's promise to us that we will receive everything that God has for us.[10] God's Spirit* will be with us until God finishes his work in us.

Still, we must continue to believe until we go to be with God. But the Holy Spirit is the promise that we will continue to believe. In Paul's letter to the church* at Philippi,* he says,

'God is the one who began his good work in you. And I am sure that he will keep on working in you until the day Jesus comes again.'[11]

It is God who saves us from the beginning to the end.

1. 2 Corinthians 5:21; Titus 3:5
2. Hebrews 8:12; Ephesians 1:7
3. Ephesians 1:4-19
4. John 3:16-18; John 5:24
5. 2 Timothy 1:12
6. Romans 8:38-39
7. John 10:27-30
8. Romans 8:28-29; Ephesians 1:3-13
9. John 8:34-36; Romans 8:21; Titus 3:3-7; John 3:9
10. Ephesians 1:13-14
11. Philippians 1:6

PART 4

Spirit* *and* Church*

091

What does God desire for all who trust* in Jesus* as Savior?*

He wants them to be holy* in heart* and in behavior. He wants them to be like Jesus.

Ephesians 1:4 • 1 Peter 1:15 • 2 Corinthians 7:1

092

How does God make us holy in heart and in behavior?

God gives us a new heart. And he gives us the Holy Spirit.*

Ezekiel 36:26 • Romans 8:1-14 • Galatians 5:22-26
Ephesians 1:13

Many years before Jesus lived, the prophet* Ezekiel* called Israel* to turn away from idols* and return to honor* God again. He talked about a day that would come in the future. God would make a new promise to Israel. He would give the people a new heart.[1] Then they would not follow other gods. They would follow God because this would be the desire of their new heart.

The word 'heart' can mean the center of anything, like the heart of a city. But most of the time, the word 'heart' speaks of the center of a person. That is not the middle of a person's body. But the center of ourselves. The heart is where we think and feel and decide. It is also the place of our wishes and desires. Our heart is where all of our actions begin, whether they are wise or foolish. Before we come to know God, our hearts are full of evil* thoughts. We do not honor God in our hearts. And it leads us to speak and do bad things. Our heart is selfish, proud, and does not look for God.[2]

When a person comes to trust Jesus, God changes his heart. Like Ezekiel told the people long ago, God 'removes our heart of stone and gives us a heart of flesh.' He compares a heart that rebels against God to stone.[3] A heart of stone cannot love God or respond to God. But when God rescues us, he gives us a heart that can respond to God. This new heart can seek God and desire to do as he asks. Now we can love the Lord* with all of our heart.

God gives us this new heart so that we can be holy. The word 'holy' means to be set apart. The scriptures* tell us that God is holy.[4] That means that God is like no other person or angel.* God is separate from any sin* or wrong or anything that is not pure.

When the word 'holy' is used for people or things, it speaks of something that is set apart for God. It means to be set apart for a special purpose. When God chose Abraham's* children to be his chosen nation, he called them to be holy. He wanted the nations near them to see that they were not like any other people. They belonged to God. When God told Moses* how to build the Tent of Worship,* he told him that the place would be holy. It would be set apart for a special purpose, a place that belonged to God. He told him to make things that would be used in this holy place. He called them holy as well. That meant that

This new heart can seek God and desire to do as he asks.

these things were to be used only in the holy place and only in the way God had said. The priests* who would serve the people were also called holy. They were the only people that could do the special things God had for them to do. They were set apart by God.

The New Testament* uses the word 'holy' to talk about the people who have believed in Jesus. When we trust Jesus, he gives us a new heart. And he sets us apart for himself. We become part of the new and holy nation of those God has chosen for himself. He gives us the Holy Spirit. And the Holy Spirit changes our hearts from having a desire to sin to having a desire to please God. So, our old hearts are changed. We love God, more and more. Our bodies are also set apart to be holy because now, the Holy Spirit lives in us. So, we act in ways that are not like the world around us. We use our bodies to show that we belong to God. We present our bodies to God.[5] We are led by the Holy Spirit to do the things he wants us to do. We learn and love God's word. We spend time with other Christians. We worship and pray with them.

We want to use our bodies to do the things that please God. When we find anything in our hearts that would not please God, we turn from it. We work to become what the Holy Spirit is changing us to be.[6] So, we work to be holy in everything we do.[7] The Holy Spirit works in our new hearts to make us more and more like God's holy Son, Jesus.

1. Ezekiel 36:26; compare Jeremiah 31:33
2. Proverbs 16:18; Jeremiah 17:9-10; Matthew 15:18-19; Romans 1:21-25
3. compare Zachariah 7:12
4. Leviticus 19:2; Isaiah 6:3; Isaiah 43:15; Revelation 4:8
5. Romans 6:13; Romans 12:1; 1 Thessalonians 4:4
6. Philippians 2:12-13
7. Hebrews 12:14; 1 Peter 1:15

question ——
093

Who is the Holy Spirit?*

The Holy Spirit is God. God the Father and God the Son sent the Holy Spirit.

Matthew 28:19 • John 14:26 • John 15:26
2 Corinthians 13:14

question ——
094

What now has the Holy Spirit become to us?

The Holy Spirit is the Comforter, the Companion, and the Guide to all who trust* in Jesus.*

John 16:7-8 • John 16:12-15 • Romans 8:14-16
1 Corinthians 6:19 • Ephesians 1:14

The Holy Spirit is God. He is one with God the Father and God the Son. He knows all things that God knows. He has all the power that God has. He is always present in all places at all times. There is no place that we can go where the Spirit* is not there.[1]

There is nothing in heaven* or on earth that the Spirit does not know.[2] Like God the Father and the Son, the Holy Spirit thinks and feels and chooses. He is a person.[3] The Holy Spirit speaks, teaches, and searches the hearts* of all people.[4] To lie to the Holy Spirit is to lie to God. The Holy Spirit is the person who is carrying out God's will in the world. He is working in such a way that God's will is being done and will be done. The Holy Spirit is active in working all things out for God's good purposes. This is true, not only in the lives of those who follow Jesus. The Holy Spirit also teaches people who do not follow Jesus. The Holy Spirit shows the people of the world the truth about sin.* He shows them what is right and what is wrong. And he tells them what it means to be judged.[5]

The Holy Spirit is the person who is carrying out God's will in the world.

When we read the Old Testament,* we find out many things about the Holy Spirit. He was there at work in creation.* He showed the prophets* what they were to say. He gave people the power to do the work that God gave them to do.[6]

The New Testament* says much more about the work of the Holy Spirit. The Holy Spirit was there when Mary* gave birth to Jesus. The Holy Spirit was there when Satan* tempted* Jesus in the desert. The Holy Spirit was with Jesus when John* baptized* him.

Jesus said many things about the Holy Spirit. He promised the disciples* that he would send the Holy Spirit to them. He said that the Spirit would come upon them after he went back to be with the Father. He called the Holy Spirit, 'the one who will come close to help.' The Spirit would always bring glory* to Jesus and he would help the disciples to do that too. Jesus promised them that they would not be alone. He would send another Counselor that would guide them, just as he had. The Holy Spirit was coming to carry on the work of Jesus. He would teach them and give them help as they did the work Jesus gave them to do.[7]

Fifty days after Jesus rose from the dead, The Holy Spirit came as Jesus promised.[8] The Spirit would give the words of Jesus to the disciples.[9] Just as the prophets spoke by the authority of the Spirit, so would the apostles.*[10] So, when the disciples spoke in the book of Acts, they spoke by the power of the Holy Spirit.

Jesus promised his disciples that the Spirit would guide them into all truth. The Holy Spirit would help them remember the things that Jesus said and did.[11] The Spirit would carry them along to help them to write what they remembered. And when they were finished, the words they had written were the very words of God.[12]

The Holy Spirit gives us new birth through the word of God. And the Spirit uses this word to make us holy.*[13]

From the start to the finish, the Holy Spirit works in us. He gives us new life as we are born into God's family. The Holy Spirit is the one who helps us to serve God. The Holy Spirit gives us wisdom when we do not know what to do. The Holy Spirit works in us to give us power to turn away from sin. He works to make us holy in what we do and what we think.[14] The Holy Spirit helps us be confident that we are God's children. He helps us trust that God has forgiven* our sins. He helps us know that we are safe forever in Christ. He comforts us when we are sad. He gives us gifts that help us serve God.

It is the Holy Spirit who gives us a desire to live a holy life. It is the Holy Spirit who helps us to trust God, who gives us faith.* It is the Holy Spirit who gives us hope.* It is the Holy Spirit who helps us see and feel God's care for us. The Holy Spirit helps us see the world and the future as God says it is and as God says it will be.

BECAUSE THE HOLY SPIRIT LIVES IN US, JESUS IS ALWAYS WITH US.

He helps us to trust in God alone. He helps us to worship* God alone, to honor* him, and to serve his glory. It is the Holy Spirit who helps us to desire God and to delight in him. He works in us so that our joy is to know God's joy. And the Holy Spirit helps us to love and delight in Jesus. Because the Holy Spirit lives in us, Jesus is always with us.[15]

1. Psalm 139:7-8
2. 1 Corinthians 2:10-11
3. Ephesians 4:30; 1 Corinthians 12:7
4. Acts 1:16; Acts 8:29; Acts 13:2; John 14:26; John 15:26; 1 Corinthians 2:11; Acts 5:3
5. John 16:8-11
6. Genesis 1:2; Psalm 33:6; Isaiah 61:1-6; Exodus 31:2-6; Judges 6:34; Judges 15:14-15

7. John 16:6-7
8. Acts 2:1-4
9. Matthew 10:20; Luke 12:12
10. John 16:13; Acts 2:4; 1 Corinthians 2:4- 5; 1 Thessalonians 1:4-5
11. John 14:26
12. 2 Timothy 3:16-17; 2 Peter 1:21
13. John 17:17; 1 Peter 1:23-25; James 1:18

14. Romans 7:6; Romans 8: 13; Philippians 1:19
15. 1 Thessalonians 1:6; 2 Corinthians 13:14; Romans 8:10; 2 Corinthians 4:6-7; Galatians 2:20; Ephesians 3:16-17; Colossians 1:27

question —— 095

How may I know the Holy Spirit* is making me Holy?*

I will grow to be more like my Savior,* Jesus* Christ.* I will see the fruit of the Spirit* in my heart* and in my behavior.

Colossians 1:9-12 • Ephesians 3:16

question —— 096

What is the fruit of the Spirit?

The fruit of the Spirit is love, joy, peace,* patience, kindness, goodness, faithfulness,* gentleness and self-control.

Galatians 5:22-23

When God chose us to be his people, his purpose was to make us like Jesus.[1] God sent His Holy Spirit to be our Helper and to do that work in us. So, when we find that we are beginning to think and act more like Jesus, we know that the Holy Spirit is at work in us. He changes us from who we were before we believed, to become who he wants us to be. The Holy Spirit does not just work to change our actions. He is at work to shape our hearts.

How does the Holy Spirit make that happen? First, the Holy Spirit helps us to turn away from the things that do not please God.[2] He works in us so that we can understand what is good and right. Then he guides us away from sinful* things. And he helps us do what is right. We still have sinful desires. But those desires grow weaker and weaker with the help of the Holy Spirit. And our desire to please God grows stronger and stronger. The Holy Spirit gives us the help we need to turn away from the sinful ways that remain in us.[3]

The Holy Spirit gives us wisdom. He makes us wise in ways that help us to understand God and what God wants us to do.[4] The Holy Spirit has given us the scriptures* to help us know these things. And the Holy Spirit uses the word of God to make us wise.[5]

Paul* lists some of the ways that the Spirit changes our hearts in a letter he wrote to a church* in Galatia.* He calls these, 'the fruit of the Spirit.' He does not use the word fruits, even though there are many things on his list. He uses the word fruit. He wants us to understand that the things on this list are all part of the same work that the Holy Spirit does. All of these things grow together.

Perhaps he uses the word fruit to tell us something else. Fruit takes time to grow. The Holy Spirit begins his work in us from the moment we believe in Jesus. And he will keep working in us to help us grow until the day when Jesus comes again.[6]

Paul starts the list of the fruit of the Spirit with love. For Paul, love is not just about how we feel about someone. When we love God, we obey him. And when we love God in this way, we will love our neighbors,* too. We will lay down our lives for them as Jesus did.[7] Jesus not only tells us to love our neighbors. He tells us to love our enemies. And we cannot love this way on our own. That is only possible when the Holy Spirit is at work in us.

The fruit of the Spirit is also joy. This is a happiness that does not depend on what happens in our lives. Joy comes to us when we understand the grace* that God has shown us. The Holy Spirit helps us see beyond what is happening now. He helps us see what God has waiting for us when Jesus comes again.

The fruit is peace. Peace is when we are free from worry or fear. We know that, even when we have troubles, God has a purpose for them. And Jesus has power over everything that troubles us.[8]

The fruit is patience. This is when the Holy Spirit helps us to keep going when life is difficult or hard. Patience helps us to show mercy* when people do wrong things to us.[9]

The fruit is kindness and goodness. Kindness comes from a heart that is gentle, a heart that shows mercy. When the Holy Spirit gives us a kind heart, we will do acts of goodness. We will not only have a good heart. We will also do good things.

The fruit is faithfulness. When we are faithful, it means that people can trust* us. Those close to us can depend on us to do what is good and right and just.

The fruit is gentleness. The Holy Spirit helps us grow in gentleness. Gentleness does not mean that the Holy Spirit wants us to be weak. To be gentle means that we are in control of ourselves. We do not allow ourselves to be angry and hurt other people. Gentleness means that we are to be strong.

The fruit is self-control. Self-control is like gentleness in some ways. It requires us to be in control of our desires. Self-control means that we are able to control our body. It means that we will not do things that will satisfy our desires in a way that would not please God.

The fruit of the Spirit in us shows that God is living in us. It is a sign to us and to those close to us that Jesus, our Lord,* is with us. And that he is working in us. The goodness, love, gentleness, peace, patience, and joy are the proof that the Holy Spirit is making us more like Jesus.

---

1. Romans 8:29;
   2 Corinthians 3:17-18;
   Colossians 3:10
2. Galatians 5:16-17; 1 Peter 5:8-9
3. 2 Corinthians 5:17;
   Philippians 4:13

4. Acts 6:9-10; 1 Corinthians 2:10-13;
   Colossians 1:9
5. John 16:13; John 17:17;
   2 Timothy 3:16-17
6. Philippians 1:6

7. John 14:15; John 14:21;
   John 14:23; John 15:12-13;
   1 John 3:16; 1 John 5:3
8. John 16:33
9. Ephesians 4:1-2; 1 Timothy 1:16

question ——
097

Will you always prosper* if you follow Jesus?*

No. I may sometimes have troubles. I may sometimes suffer or be hated just as Jesus was.

John 15:18-19 • 2 Timothy 3:12 • Romans 8:23-25
James 1:2-4 • 1 Peter 4:12-13

question ——
098

How does God help you in times of trouble?

He gives me the Spirit* to comfort me. He gives me the church* to care for me. He gives me his promise to work in all things for my good and for his glory.*

Romans 5:3-5 • Romans 8:18 • 1 Thessalonians 5:11
1 Peter 4:12-19 • 1 Peter 5:10

When we trust* Jesus, God becomes our Father.[1] God welcomes us into his family. He promises to care for us. He shows us his care by blessing* us in many ways. Human fathers know how to give good gifts to their children. So does our Father in heaven.* He forgives us. He gives us his Holy Spirit.* He gives us wisdom and makes us new people. These are wonderful gifts. They are all from the hand of God. And God has given these gifts to men and women, slave and free, the rich and the poor.[2] All these gifts come to us because he gave us the gift of his son, Jesus.[3]

Some people think if we had God's full blessing, we would also have lots of money. We would never be sick. And we would always be happy.

But the scriptures* do not say this. Jesus did not say this. None of the men who wrote the New Testament* say this.

And Jesus did not tell poor people that they were poor because God was not pleased with them. Jesus himself became poor so that he could do the work God sent him to do. James* said that many people who are poor are rich in faith.*[4]

Money is not always a sign that God has blessed* us. Jesus told people to be careful not to love money. He warned people not to depend on money, because it does not last. Instead, we must depend on God who is the same forever.

Jesus said that wanting to be rich can make it hard for a person to follow him. Jesus and the men who wrote the New Testament warn us that money can be a bad thing for us. James warned the rich that their desire for more money was keeping them from God's blessing. Paul* said that if we love money, it can lead us into all kinds of evil.* God wants his people to be free from the love of money.[5]

Jesus did not promise his followers* an easy life. He said they would have troubles. Jesus told the men who followed him that people would hate them. They would hate them because they hated Jesus first. We know that Jesus and most of the people who followed him suffered many troubles. Peter* was put in prison. Stephen* was killed. People threw stones at Paul until they thought he was dead. They did this because these men loved and followed Jesus. These men did not have trouble because they did not trust God. They suffered because they did trust him.

But Jesus also promised great rewards to his people. Paul and Peter both said that when Jesus comes again, all of God's riches will be ours. But those blessings come to us in heaven. A new heaven and a new earth will be our new home. And what God gives us there cannot be taken away.

So, if we do have troubles as Jesus and his followers did, how does God help us in our troubles?

God is with us in our pain. God has given us his Holy Spirit. He is our helper who gives us comfort. The Holy Spirit helps us to know that we are God's children, and that God is a good Father.

God has also made us a part of a new family. We are a part of the church, the family of God's people. God put us in this family so that we can find help and so that we can be a help to other people. God wants us to comfort other people who have the same troubles. We give them the same kind of comfort that God gives us.[6] He puts us in the church so that we can love one another. Encourage one another. And bear one another's troubles. In the company of the people of God, we will find help in times of trouble.

God is with us in our pain.

It is a comfort to remember that God is in control of all things. He controls all that he created.* He controls the wind and the seas. He controls the nations. And He works all things, even our troubles, for His good purposes and for our good. Paul had an illness, but God used the illness to help Paul trust God more. Paul was beaten and shipwrecked. People tried to kill him. But he says this was all a part of God's plan to spread the gospel.*[7]

Not everything that happens to us is good. But God uses even the bad things, as part of His good plan for us.[8]

Nothing can come against us that can ever separate us from God's love for us. And no bad thing can come into our lives that can keep God from doing his work in us.

———

NOTHING CAN COME AGAINST US THAT CAN EVER SEPARATE US FROM GOD'S LOVE FOR US.

———

1. Romans 8:15
2. Galatians 3:14; Galatians 3:28
3. John 3:16-18; 2 Corinthians 9:15
4. Luke 9:58; 2 Corinthians 8:9; Philippians 2:6-8; James 2:5

5. Matthew 6:19-24; Luke 1:18; Luke 12:15; Ephesians 5:5-7; 1 Timothy 3:3; 1 Timothy 6:10; Hebrews 13:5
6. 2 Corinthians 1:3-5

7. Acts 9:16; 2 Corinthians 11:24-27
8. Isaiah 46:10; Romans 8:28; Ephesians 3:20

question ——
099

What is the universal Church?*

The universal Church is made up of all of God's redeemed* people. The Church* is the family of God the Father. It is the body of Christ* the Son. It is the place where the Holy Spirit* lives.

1 Corinthians 12:27 • Ephesians 3:14-15
Ephesians 5:23 • Colossians 1:24 • Hebrews 2:11

Jesus is the Messiah.* God promised that he would come to rescue Israel.* But he did not come to save Israel only. He came to save the whole world.[1] God promised Abraham* that, through his family, all of the families of the world would be blessed.*[2] This family of Abraham is now called the church. The word 'church' comes from a Greek word that means to gather together.

The church is a group of people who are called to gather together. God has set apart those who have put their trust* in Jesus. He calls them to gather together as his Holy Nation,[3] as Peter* calls them.

The word 'universal' means something that applies to all people. So, the universal Church is made up of all believers* in Jesus Christ in all parts of the world. People also use the words universal church to speak of anyone who has ever or will ever believe in Jesus. So, it is the people God has called to himself in the past, the present, and the future.

When we use the word church in this way, we are not talking about something that Christians do. We do not speak of the church meeting. We speak of who we are. We, who believe in Jesus, are the church. We are the church all of the time, everywhere we go. We are the church when we are together and when we are alone. We are the church when we are all in one place. And we are the church when we are scattered in many places.

The New Testament* calls the universal Church, the Body of Christ.[4]

When Jesus came into the world he came in a body of flesh and blood. In that body, Jesus showed us who God is. And he showed us how much God loves us when he died on the cross* in our place. Now Christ is in heaven,* in his body that God raised from the dead.

But Jesus is still at work in the world. He is doing his work through the people that he has called to be his own. So, the church is now the body of Christ on earth. He uses our hands to do his work. He uses our voices to speak kind words to people who are hurting. He uses our feet to go into all the world to take his good news to all people. Jesus does this work in us with the help of the Holy Spirit.

The Holy Spirit came to live in us when we believed that Jesus is the Messiah. The Spirit* gives us the wisdom and power to do the work Jesus wants us to do. That is why the New Testament calls our body 'the temple* of the Holy Spirit.' The temple in the Old Testament* was the place where God came to be present among his people.

After Jesus came, and rose from the dead, he sent his Holy Spirit to live in all of the people who trust him. So now, our bodies are his temple, because God lives in us. And the Holy Spirit lives in everyone who is part of the church. So each of us is the temple of the Holy Spirit. And all of us together are the temple of the Holy Spirit. God is present in the world, in the church, the body of Christ, and the temple of the Holy Spirit.[5] Paul* tells us that since we are the temple, we should be people who live for God's glory.* We should honor* God in all that we do.

The scriptures* also say that the church is the family of God. When we believed on God's son, we became a child of God.[6] God adopted* us so that we could be one of his own dear children. God is our Father, and he welcomes us into his family. Now we can call him Father.[7]

We are no longer strangers to God. We are his sons and daughters. So, all who are part of the church belong to the same family. We are not alone. We have brothers and sisters in every nation. They speak every language from every tribe.*[8] But we are all one family together.

1. John 1:11-12; John 3:17; John 12:44-47
2. Genesis 12:2; Genesis 17:4; Genesis 18:18
3. 1 Peter 2:9
4. Romans 12:5; 1 Corinthians 10:7; 1 Corinthians 12:27; Ephesians 4:12; Ephesians 5:23; Colossians.1:24
5. 1 Corinthians 3:16; 1 Corinthians 6:19
6. John 1:12
7. Ephesians 1:15
8. Revelation 5:9; Revelation 7:9

question —— 100

What is the local church?*

The local church* is a group of people that trust* in Jesus* Christ* and obey his commands. They worship* God together. They hear and learn the scriptures* together. They care for each other and are cared for. They pray and work together to see God's kingdom* grow. They baptize* believers* and eat the Lord's* Supper.

Matthew 28:19-20 • Acts 2:41-42 • Acts 8:36-39
Acts 14:23 • Romans 6:1-5 • 1 Corinthians 11:23-26
Titus 1:5

question —— 101

Should I be a part of a local church?

Yes. The local church is the community* that helps me grow and stay strong in my faith.* It is where I learn to obey Jesus' new command.

Hebrews 10:24-25

When the word 'church' is used to talk about people who meet in a place, we call this a 'local church.' Sometimes the word was used for a small group of believers who would meet in one place, like a house. At other times, the word was used to talk about all of the believers in a city. So we hear Paul* talk about the church in Corinth.* That is, all of the believers who were meeting in the many different places in the city of Corinth.¹ The local church can also mean many groups in a larger area, like the churches in Judea and Galilee and Samaria.*²

What is the local church like? Luke* tells us many things about what the first church in Jerusalem* was like. He wrote this so that we could see how a local church is supposed to act.³

First, the church listened to what the Apostles* taught them. These were the closest followers* of Jesus. Before Jesus went to the cross*, he promised to give these men the Holy Spirit.* Then he told them that the Holy Spirit would help them remember what Jesus had said and done. Over the next years, God used these men and other men whom the Apostles taught to write the New Testament* scriptures. The Holy Spirit guided them as they wrote. The words of these Apostles would guide the church. The church believed that what the scripture said was what God himself had said. So, they listened with great care to what the Apostles taught.

The people in the first church in Jerusalem also shared their lives together. They helped those who were poor among them. And they cared for each other. Luke says that they shared everything that they owned.

The church also came together to pray. They prayed for one another. They prayed for the Holy Spirit to help them know what God wanted them to do. They asked God to provide them with the things that they needed. They prayed that God would protect them. They prayed that many people would hear the good news about Jesus and would believe it.[4]

Luke says that they 'broke bread' together. They shared meals together. We also know that they ate the Lord's Supper together. The night before Jesus died, he shared a meal with his disciples.* In that meal, he broke bread and gave it to them. They also drank with him from the cup he gave them. He said that taking the bread and the cup was a sign and that they should do this when they met together. This would help them remember what he had done for them on the cross.

Luke also says, that whenever they met, they gave praise* to God. We know that sometimes they did this by telling what God had done for them. They would also sing together. Sometimes they would speak to one another with the words of the Psalms* that they knew.[5]

The church is also where we learn. We learn the scriptures so that we can become wise. And because we learn together with other Christians,* they help us to live in a way that pleases God.[6]

Many people in Jerusalem saw what the church was doing, and they listened to what the Apostles were saying. Because of that, many people believed in Jesus. And just as John the Baptist* had baptized Jesus, the church baptized all of those who believed.

When we believe in Jesus, we must find a place where those who believe in Jesus meet. We should join with other believers in a local church. The writer of the book of Hebrews* says that we should not stay away from meeting with other believers.[7] When we meet, this is where we love and help each other. We can use our gifts that God has given us to serve other people. And we can comfort those who have problems and remind each other to do what is good.

We should not stay away from meeting with other believers.

Sadly, not every church does the same things that the first church did. They meet and teach. But some do not teach what the scriptures say. We are to listen to the teachers in the church who teach the word of God to us. But we must not listen to anyone who teaches anything that is not from scripture. If a church teaches things that neither Jesus, or any of the apostles or prophets* taught, it is not a true church. When we find ourselves in a place like that, we must pray that God will help us find a church that will teach and honor* the truth.[8]

1. 1 Corinthians 1:12
2. Acts 9:31
3. Acts 2:42-47
4. Matthew 6:13; John 17:20-21;
   Romans 10:1; Ephesians 1:17;
   Ephesians 3:19;
   2 Thessalonians 3:1

5. Ephesians 5:19; Colossians 3:16
6. Hebrews 13:7; Hebrews 13:17;
   1 John 5:14-15; 1 Timothy 2:8;
   Ephesians 6:16-18; James 5:16;
   Philippians 1:15-18;
   Galatians 2:11-16;
   Colossians 1:21-23

7. Hebrews 10:24-25
8. 1 Timothy 3:15

102

What is the new command that Jesus* gave to the church?*

Jesus said, 'Love each other. You must love each other as I have loved you.'

John 13:34

103

How may we show this love for one another?

We show this love when we are kind to each other, pray for each other, and forgive* each other. We show this love when we honor* each other, help each other, and encourage each other. We show this love when we speak the truth to each other and put each other's needs before our own.

Romans 12:10 • Ephesians 4:32 • Colossians 3:9
Colossians 3:13 • 1 Thessalonians 4:18 • James 5:16

Before Jesus went to the cross,* he met with his disciples.* He told them many things that would happen to him. He told them that he was going away. He told them that he would send the Holy Spirit* to help them. He gave them a new command to love each other.

'You must love each other as I have loved you.'

The first part of the command was not new. God had told his people to love their neighbors.* He gave that command to Moses* many years before Jesus lived. But now, Jesus says that those who follow him must love one another as Jesus has loved them. Just as Jesus had served them, they would need to serve each other. Jesus loved them. Now they would need to love one another.

Jesus gave that command to a small group of men who ate with him the night before he died. But they understood that this was a command for anyone who would follow Jesus. When the Apostles* wrote their letters to the churches, they reminded them of Jesus' command many times.[1] The church was to be a place where people loved other people as Jesus had loved them.

This was an important thing to say to these new churches. Most of the churches had started with Jews* as the only members. But soon, many men and women who were not Jews began to believe in Jesus. In the Old Testament*, the Jews did not mix with people from other nations. They followed the one, true God while the people who were not Jews worshipped* idols.* Only Jews could go into the holy places in the Temple.* So, the Jews were separate from people who were not Jews.

But now, the Gentiles* were part of the new, holy* people that God had chosen. They did not know many of the laws* that God had given the Jews. So, in the beginning of the church, the Jews did not always know how to welcome these new believers* and accept them as brothers and sisters. But the Holy Spirit helped the Apostles to understand what to say about this problem.

So how can we show love to one another? The Apostles answered that question in many places in the New Testament.*[2]

There, the scriptures* tell us to be people who are at peace* with one another.[3] We are not to argue with each other or complain about what God is doing in our world. We are to show patience with one another and serve each other. We are not to envy each other or boast about ourselves. Instead, we are to be patient, gentle, and kind. If we hurt someone, we must work to correct the wrong that we have done. And if someone hurts us, we must not hurt them. We must forgive them and try to understand them.

We must ask God to help us become people who can love one another. We must ask God to make us humble and not proud. We must serve other people rather than expecting them to serve us. We must not lie to each other but speak the truth. We are to encourage one another. We are not to be people who judge and find fault with each other. We must be people who build each other up. We must never forget to pray for one another.

We cannot do these things or be this kind of people without the Holy Spirit to help us. But because he is in us and is at work in us, we can follow Jesus' new command. When we love each other, the people close to us will know that we are followers* of Jesus. And when they see what God has done in us, God may use that to bring them to Jesus too.

---

1. Romans 13:10; 1 Thessalonians 4:9; 1 Peter 1:22; 1 John 3:2; 1 John 4:11
2. John 13:34; John 15:12; John 15:17; Romans 13:8; Romans 14:13; Galatians 5:13; Galatians 6:2; Ephesians 4:25; Ephesians 4:32; Philippians 2:3; Colossians 3:9; Colossians 3:13; 1 Thessalonians 3:12; 1 Thessalonians 5:11; 1 Thessalonians 5:15; Hebrews 10:24; James 4:11, James 5:9; James 5:16; 1 Peter 4:9; 1 Peter 5:5; 1 John 3:11; 1 John 4:7; 2 John 5
3. Mark 9:50; John 6:43

question 104

What is Baptism?*

In baptism a church* leader puts a person under water for a moment. Then the person is brought up out of the water. They do this in the name of the Father, the Son, and the Holy Spirit.*

Matthew 3:6,16 • Mark 1:5 • Acts 8:12

question 105

Who can be baptized?*

Baptism is foreveryone who repents* of their sins.* It is for all those who believe in Christ* for salvation.*

Acts 2:38-39 • Acts 8:36-37 • Acts 16:30-33

question 106

What does baptism mean?

Baptism is a sign of the believer's* unity with Christ when he died, was buried and was raised from the dead. It says that I am part of his church.

Acts 16:30-33 • Romans 6:3-5 • Colossians 2:12

In some places in the world, when two people marry, they put on a ring. The ring is a sign. It shows other people that these two people have made promises to one another. They had already made the promises in their hearts.* But when they put on the rings, they were saying that they will keep their promise. Everyone who sees the ring knows that it is more than a simple ring. That ring is the sign that this person has promised themselves to someone.

For the person who follows Jesus,* baptism is the sign. It is the sign of a promise to follow Jesus.

We do not read about anyone being baptized in the Old Testament.* But, in the New Testament,* we know that Jews* sometimes baptized people in the time Jesus lived. Sometimes a person who was not a Jew wanted to become a Jew or follow the ways that the Jews followed. So, the Jews taught this person for a long time. When the teaching was finished, they would baptize the person. This was a sign that they were clean and could now go to the Temple.* But it was also a sign to show that what they used to be, was put behind them. Now, they are a new person. It was a sign that they had left one life and were starting a new one.

Why do Christian churches baptize people? Just before Jesus left his disciples* to go to heaven,* he gave a command. He said that they should take the good news about Jesus to all of the world. He also told them to baptize the people who believed the message. Then they were to teach those people all that Jesus had taught them. Christians baptize those who believe because Jesus told them to.[1] Christians* baptize in order to please and obey Christ.

Who should be baptized? In the book of Acts, Luke* tells us about the first message that Peter* spoke. He was with a crowd

218 | SPIRIT AND CHURCH

of people. He told them who Jesus was and why he had come. When they heard the message, their hearts were troubled because of their sin. So, they asked Peter and the other apostles,*

> 'What should we do?' Peter said, 'Repent and be baptized.'

Later, in Acts, a man named Philip* was telling people about Jesus. After they heard the good news, many of them put their trust in Jesus. Then Philip baptized them.[2] Who should be baptized? The answer is, all of those who repent and put their trust* in Jesus.[3]

What does baptism mean? Paul writes to the Romans* that baptism is a picture of what happens to us when we come to Jesus. First, we go into the water. This shows that, when Jesus died, our old life died there with Jesus. When we are under the water, our old life is buried with Jesus. When we come up from the water, it is a picture that, in Jesus, we are rising to a new life.[4] Death could not keep Jesus in the grave. So, our baptism is a picture that death cannot hold us either. God will raise us from death just as he raised the body of Jesus.

After God raised Jesus from the dead, everyone who believed in Jesus was baptized. All of the members of the first church were people who believed and were baptized.

Baptism is the way we show people that we have believed in Jesus. It is a sign to everyone who sees us that we have repented. We have believed. And we have become part of God's family.

---

1. Matthew 28:18-20
2. Acts 9:26-40

3. Acts 2:37-38; Acts 8:4-12
4. Romans 6:3-4

question ——
107

How do Christians* remind each other about Jesus'* death for them?

We share in the Lord's* Supper together.

Mark 14:22-24 • 1 Corinthians 11:23-29

question ——
108

What is the Lord's Supper?

At the Lord's Supper we eat bread and drink the cup. We do this to remember the death of Jesus Christ.*

Mark 14:22-24 • 1 Corinthians 11:23-29

In the Old Testament,* God gave his people signs to help them remember important things. Sometimes, he gave them a sign to help them remember something that he had done for them. Or God gave them a sign to help them remember what he had promised them.

In the days that Noah* lived, God sent a flood. The flood covered the whole earth. But before the flood came, God told Noah to build a boat. He was to take his family and many animals with him into the boat. Noah built the boat and gathered the animals. Then, God sent the flood. After the waters from the flood were gone, Noah and his family and all of the animals came out of the boat. God saved them from the flood. And God made a promise to Noah. He promised that he would never again send this kind of flood on the earth. And then God gave Noah a sign of this promise. God put a rainbow in the sky. He told Noah that, every time he saw the rainbow, he was to remember God's promise.[1]

Many years after Noah, the twelve tribes* of Israel* stood by a river. These tribes were born from the children of Abraham.* And on the other side of the river was the land that God had promised to give Abraham. Before they crossed the river, God made the river stop so that the people could go across on dry ground. But before they went across, Joshua,* their leader, told one man from every tribe to pick up a stone from the dry river. They were to carry these stones across the river with them. When they got to the other side and stopped to rest, they were to put these stones on top of one another. Then Joshua said,

'When your children ask what these stones mean, tell them that God stopped the river. And we walked into this land on dry ground.'

The stones would cause the people to remember what God had done.[2]

The night before Jesus went to the cross,* he ate a meal with his disciples.* It was the meal that God gave the people of Israel when they came out of the land of Egypt.* God had done many great things to bring the people out of Egypt. But before they left there, God told them to make a special meal. They would eat special food and prepare everything just as he told them to. Then, God told them why he gave them the meal. God said,

'You will eat this meal on this day. For on this day, I brought you out of the land of Egypt. So, all of you will remember this day forever.'[3]

As Jesus and the disciples were eating, he told them that he was going to be handed over to be killed. Then, Jesus took bread. When he had broken it, he gave it to his disciples. And he said that the bread was like his body. And he told them to eat it and said, 'Do this to remember me.' Then he took a cup of wine and said that the wine was like his blood. And he told them to drink. Then he told them that, when they ate this bread and drank from this cup, they should remember that he died for them.[4]

Ever since that time, followers* of Jesus have been eating this meal to remember Jesus. The meal has become known as the Lord's Supper. Like the signs God gave Noah and Joshua, when we eat this bread and drink from this cup, we are to remember. We remember what Jesus did for us when he died on the cross. We remember how much he loved us. He forgave our sins and gave us eternal* life. And we remember the promises Jesus made to those who follow him. He said that he would forgive* all who trust* in him. He promised that he would never turn anyone away who comes to him. He promised he would help us every day. He promised that, if we are tired and carry a heavy load, he will give us rest. He promised he would never leave us alone. And he will raise us up from death and give us a life that lasts forever.[5]

---

1. Genesis 9:1-17
2. Joshua 4:1-7
3. Exodus 12:1-17

4. Matthew 26:26-30; Mark 14:22-26; Luke 22:14-20; 1 Corinthians 11:26

5. Matthew 11:28; John 3:15-18; John 3:36; John 6:37-39

question —— 109

What does the bread mean?

The broken bread speaks about the broken body of Christ.* He died once because of our sins.*

Matthew 26:26 • 1 Corinthians 11:24

question —— 110

What does the cup mean?

The cup speaks about the blood of Christ. He bled once for our salvation.*

Matthew 26:27-28 • 1 Corinthians 11:25

When we want to tell someone about our children, sometimes, we show them a picture. We hold up the picture so that they can see. Then we point and say, 'This is my boy. And this one is my girl.' When we say this, we do not mean that our child is an image on a piece of paper. We mean this is a picture of my daughter. That is a picture of my son. My children look like this.

Jesus* gave his disciples* bread and said, 'This is my body.' He gave them wine to drink and said, 'This is the blood that brings a new promise.' Just as we use a picture to show people our children, Jesus used the bread and the cup. They were pictures of what Jesus was about to do for them. They were pictures of his death for us.

A few hours after they ate this meal, Jesus was with his disciples. Roman* soldiers came to where they were and took Jesus away. The soldiers took Jesus to the leaders of the Jews.* These leaders told lies about what Jesus had done. Those men would say that Jesus had broken the laws* of the Jews. They said that Jesus had said bad things about God. So, they asked the Roman leaders to punish him. And they did.

They beat Jesus with a whip made from the skin of an animal. This hurt Jesus very badly. It cut his body and made him bleed. They hit him with their hands and with sticks. They spit on Jesus and hit him on the head again and again. They said bad things to him. They made a crown for his head made from sharp thorns. Then they pressed it hard on his head. The thorns went into his skin. They took his clothes away from him. Then they made him carry a heavy cross.

They made him walk to a hill outside of Jerusalem.* Then they nailed his body to the cross.* They pushed large nails into his hands and his feet. Then they stood the cross up straight and Jesus hung there in front of them. People laughed at him as he suffered.

He hung there for many hours. And when he had cried out in a loud voice, he died. The Roman soldiers put a sharp spear into his side and water mixed with blood poured out.[1]

The disciples did not stay with him when he was on the cross. They did not understand what was happening. The disciples did not know how the Messiah* could go through a terrible death and be put to shame. They had watched Jesus die and all of their hope* had died too.

But after God raised Jesus from the dead, they began to understand. And later the Holy Spirit* would help them remember the things he had said to them. Jesus had said that he had the power over his life. No one could take his life from him. He could lay his life down and he could take it up again. And he said that he was like a shepherd.* And he was going to give his life for his sheep.[2] Jesus went to the cross to take the punishment for our sins. He gave himself as a sacrifice* to end all of God's anger against us.[3]

When we eat the bread and drink from the cup, we are to remember this. We must always thank God for forgiving* us and giving us life. This came to us as a free gift.[4] But the cost of this gift was very high. To give us this gift, Jesus had to suffer and die. He took our punishment. He gave us the gift we could not earn.

God raised Jesus from the dead.

In the Old Testament,* when a person sinned,* they could bring an animal to the priests. The priests would kill the lamb* to make a sacrifice. The animal had to die so that the one who sinned could go free and be forgiven.* But then people would do more bad things. And more animals would need to be killed. But when Jesus became a sacrifice for us, no more animals would ever need to be killed. Jesus made a perfect sacrifice. God the Father looked on that sacrifice and was pleased – once and for all.[5]

---

1. Matthew 27:27-50; John 19:34
2. Matthew 20:19; Matthew 26:2; John 10:11-18
3. Romans 3:5; Romans 5:9; 1 John 2:2; 1 John 4:10
4. Romans 6:23; Romans 8:32; Ephesians 2:8-9
5. Isaiah 53:11; Hebrews 9:26-28

question ——

111

Who should eat the Lord's* Supper?

The Lord's Supper is foreveryone who repents* of their sins.* It is for all those who believe in Christ* for salvation.*

1 Corinthians 10:16-17 • 1 Corinthians 11:18-29

question ——

112

Who gave baptism* and the Lord's Supper to the church?*

The Lord Jesus* Christ.

Matthew 26:26-29 • Matthew 28:18-20

question ——

113

Why did Jesus Christ give baptism and the Lord's Supper to the church?

Jesus Christ gave these to show that his people belong to him. These acts remind us of what Jesus has done for us.

Matthew 28:19 • Romans 6:1-5
1 Corinthians 11:23-26

After God raised Jesus from the dead, Jesus' followers* began to tell people the good news. This news travelled to many places very far from Jerusalem* where it all started. Soon, people in the city of Corinth* heard the news and many people believed. The believers* began to gather, and a church grew up there. After many years, Paul* decided that he should write a letter to the church there. They were having some problems and Paul wanted to help them. Some of the people there were not acting in a good way when the church ate the Lord's Supper. So that is one of the things he talked about in his letter.

Paul reminded them where the meal came from and why it is important.

He told them that on the night before Jesus died, he took bread. He gave thanks to God and then broke some bread for his disciples* to eat. It was Jesus who first ate this meal with the disciples. So he told them what to do. Jesus said,

'Take this bread and eat it. This is my body which is broken for you. Do this to remember me.'

Jesus also took the cup and gave it to them to drink from. He said,

'This cup brings a new promise between you and God by My blood. Whenever you drink it, do it to remember me.'

When Jesus first ate this meal with his followers, he made them a promise. He said that he was going away. But he would drink it with them again one day as they sit together in his Father's kingdom.*[1]

Paul says, 'This means that you are to eat this bread and drink from this cup. And every time that you do, you are telling of the Lord's death until he comes again. But you should look into your own heart* before you eat the bread and drink from the cup. You must not forget how Jesus gave his body for you. If you do, this will not please God.'

Paul wants the Lord's Supper to be important to them. He wants them to take care of one another as they eat. So, he writes to help them. He says, when they eat, they are to think about what Jesus did for them. Jesus gave his body to rescue them. And they should remember that Jesus is coming again. And they will stand before him when he comes. Paul tells them that, if they think about these things, they will honor* God as they eat.[2]

We do not come to eat the Lord's Supper because we think that the bread and the cup will save us. We come to honor Jesus because he has already saved us. We come because we believe that Jesus has done all that God has required. We come to the supper because we are part of his family and he welcomes us there. We come because we love him. We are so thankful for what he did for us.

Jesus gave us the Lord's Supper to help us so that we would not forget that he loves us.[3] He loves us so much that he put himself into the hands of men who caused him to suffer. He died a painful death to rescue us so that we would not have to suffer such a death.

We were weak and could not help ourselves. God showed His love to us. While we were still sinners,* Christ died for us. Christ came at the right time and gave his life for people who did not please God. God saved us from the punishment of sin by the blood of Christ. He has also saved us from God's anger. We were enemies of God. But we were saved from the punishment of sin by the death of Christ. And because he rose again to life, even when we were far away, he brought us back to God.[4]

---

1. Matthew 26:27-29
2. 1 Corinthians 11:23-28
3. Romans 8:38-39; 1 John 4:7-11; 1 John 4:16-19
4. Romans 5:6-11

114

What was Christ's* last command on earth to his Church?*

'All authority in heaven* and on earth has been given to me. So, go and make disciples* of all nations. Baptize* them in the name of the Father and of the Son and of the Holy Spirit.* Teach them to obey everything that I have commanded you. And you can be sure that I am always with you, to the very end.'

Matthew 28:18-20

Jesus* was alive again! His disciples saw him. Peter* saw him. Mary Magdalene* saw him. More than 500 people saw him too. And he stayed and taught his disciples for 40 days. Just before he went back to be with the Father, he met with his disciples on a mountain. As they listened, Jesus gave them this command.

He tells them what he wants them to do after he leaves them and after he sends the Holy Spirit. But first, he tells them that God the Father has given him authority over all things. He rules all things in heaven and on the earth. He wants them to know that he has everything under his control and he rules it all. There is not one place in heaven or on earth where he is not King.[1]

JESUS WAS ALIVE AGAIN!

So, what he is going to say comes as a command. But it also gives them confidence. They are going to do what he asks as people who are carrying out the orders of the King. And he gives them authority and power to do what he commands.

A few days later, Jesus would send them the Holy Spirit. The Spirit* would give them the power to do what Jesus commands. They would be able to tell people about Jesus. They would start with the people who were close to them. Then they would take the good news about Jesus from one end of the earth to the other.

So, Jesus' command is to go and make disciples. A disciple is a person that follows and learns from someone. Jesus called men and women to follow him and learn from him. Now the men and women who followed him are to call people to follow Jesus. Jesus is now going to do his work through his disciples and the Holy Spirit will help them.

Jesus tells them that they must baptize these new disciples and then teach them. When people hear the good news about Jesus and believe in him, they are to be baptized. This is the sign to all who see it that this man or woman has decided to follow Jesus. This is the first step in becoming a disciple of Jesus: repent* and believe.

Then Jesus tells the disciples to teach new believers* all that Jesus had told them. And he wanted them to show new believers how to obey those things.

As we read the scriptures,* we find out how the disciples did this. Those who had been with Jesus taught other men and women. And they learned how to put these things into practice as they shared their lives together. They learned and 'helped each other to love other people and do good.'[2] All that they learned, they put into practice in their lives. They did this as a community.*

Jesus' command is for us too. Every follower* of Jesus must share Jesus everywhere he or she goes. And we do not only share the news. We are to urge and encourage people to believe it. When they do, they become a part of the community of Christ followers. When we help people learn to follow Jesus, we are not only to teach what Jesus said. We must also teach them to know how to live the way Jesus lived.

Jesus wanted them to see that they were to take the gospel* to every nation. This does not only mean to the nations that we can see on a map. It means to every group of people. When John* wrote the last book of the Bible,* he told us about a vision* that God gave him. God showed him many things that would happen in the future. In this dream, he saw a great crowd of people. There were so many that he could not count them. These were all of the people who had believed in Jesus. And John says that there were people there 'from every nation and from every tribe* and from every kind of people and from every language.' Jesus wants all people everywhere to hear the good news and come to him.[3]

What Jesus told us to do will not be easy. When we live for him and speak for him, some people will not welcome us. Some may even hate us and make things difficult for us. But Jesus says that we are not to let this stop us. And we are not to worry. He will be with us everywhere we go, in this life and in the life to come.

---

1. Ephesians 1:19-23; Philippians 2:8-11; Revelation 17:14

2. Hebrews 10:24-25

3. Revelation 7:9

question 115

What is the Lord's* Day?

The Lord's Day is the first day of the week. The early Christians* gathered on that day.

Acts 20:7 • 1 Corinthians 16:2 • Revelation 1:10

question 116

Why is it called the Lord's Day?

Because on that day Christ* rose from the dead.

Matthew 28:1-6 • Luke 24:1-6 • John 20:1

question 117

How may we best spend the Lord's day?

We best spend the Lord's Day when we gather with God's people to worship him and encourage each other in our faith.*

Psalm 27:4 • Romans 12:9-13 • Colossians 3:16

Before Jesus* came, the Jews* worshipped God on the last day of the week. That day was called the Sabbath.* It was one of the ten commands that God put on the tables made of stone and gave to Moses.* It said,

'Remember the Sabbath and keep it as a holy day.'

On that day, they were to remember that God had brought them out from Egypt.*[1] The Sabbath began Friday at sunset and ended Saturday at sunset. This was to be a day of complete rest from all work. It helped them remember that the Creator* rested on the seventh day.[2] The Sabbath was a special sign to the people of Israel* that they had been set apart as followers* of the one, true God.

But the Sabbath Day was not a day when God's people went to a meeting to worship. It was a day of rest. When Moses and the prophets* spoke of the Sabbath, they spoke of it as a day to rest.[3] There is no command to meet to worship on that day. Rest from work is what made the Sabbath special time.

In those days, the way that people were to honor* God was to go to the Tent of Meeting or to the Temple.* God gave Moses many instructions on how the people were to worship there. Most of the people lived too far away from the Tent of Meeting or the Temple to go to worship there every Sabbath day. The Sabbath was kept at home, by resting. It was a way that Israel could show that they did not trust* their own work to feed them and bring them good things. Their rest was a way to show that they trusted God and rested in him.

But after the Babylonian* army took many Jews from their land, Jews began to build what they called synagogues.* The Jews were scattered and lived in many nations. So, they built synagogues where there were enough of their people to gather together and remember that they were God's chosen people. They would read the law* together and talk about it there. They met to encourage one another and remind one another about God's promises to Abraham* and to David* and to them. They met on many different days in the synagogue. But the most important meeting was on the Sabbath.

After Jesus rose from the dead, the apostles* still spoke of the Sabbath.* Many of the new Christians were Jews. They kept going to the synagogue as they did before. When Paul* went to a new place, he told people about Jesus. He would often begin by telling the people in the synagogue.

As the church* grew, many of the new believers* were not Jews. They did not go to a synagogue. They had never rested on the Sabbath as a way to honor God. They had never followed the laws that God gave to Moses for the children of Abraham. So, it became a practice for the church of new believers to gather on Sunday, the first day of the week. This was the day when Jesus rose from the dead. It was called the 'Lord's Day.' Since that time, believers have gathered on the first day of the week. They gather to worship Jesus and give thanks for his victory over sin* and death.[5]

Some people have called the Lord's Day, the Christian Sabbath. We can see why they do that. The Jews were to honor God by resting on the Sabbath. And new Christians chose the Lord's day to honor God. When the Jews built the synagogues, they did many of the same kinds of things there that the early Christians did as the church. But nowhere in the Scripture* is the Sabbath ever called the Lord's Day or the Lord's Day called the Sabbath.

The words, 'Lord's Day' are only used once in the New Testament.* John* wrote in his letter that the Holy Spirit* spoke to him in a special way on the Lord's Day. He did not need to explain what he meant when he used those words. So, it seems that the people he wrote to already knew what the Lord's Day was.

Meeting together to worship and learn and care for one another is important. The first people who trusted in Jesus did this every day. They gathered in houses and meeting places. But it seems that the first day of the week became an important day. The early

Christians made it a habit to meet together as the church on that day. They listened to the apostles teach. They honored God in worship. They ate together, gave gifts to help the poor, and cared for one another.

Wise Christians still use this day to gather as the church. We must make it our habit to meet together with believers. And we must not stop meeting together.[6] But it is not a law as the Sabbath was for the Jews. We are not welcomed by Jesus because we keep rules. We must encourage one another and love one another. Jesus is our rest, our peace,* and our hope.* So, we must not judge one another about what day we gather to worship.[7]

1. Deuteronomy 5:15
2. Genesis 2:2-3; Exodus 20:11; Exodus 23:12
3. Exodus 31:12-17, Numbers 15:32, Nehemiah 13:15-22; Jeremiah 17:19-27
4. Matthew 12:5; John 7:23; Colossians 2:16
5. Acts 20:7; 1 Corinthians 16:2
6. Hebrews 10:25
7. Romans 3:28; Colossians 2:16-17; Hebrews 4:9-11

—

JESUS IS OUR REST, OUR PEACE, AND OUR HOPE.

—

Prayer *and* Hope*

question 118

What is prayer?

Prayer is when we talk to God. We thank him for his goodness. We confess* our sin.* We ask for things that please him.

Matthew 6:6 • Philippians 4:6 • 1 John 5:14

question 119

In whose name should we pray?

We should pray in the name of Jesus.*

John 14:13-14 • John 16:23

question 120

When and where should we pray?

We can pray to God anywhere and at any time.

Matthew 6:6 • Ephesians 6:18 • Acts 21:5
Colossians 4:2

All people who go to a place of worship,* pray. Muslims* pray. Jewish* people pray. Buddhists pray. People who believe in one God pray. People who believe in many gods pray. Some people pray to the spirits of animals. Some people pray to the spirits of their ancestors.* Some pray and believe that God is listening. Some pray but do not believe that anyone is listening.

Christians believe in a God who speaks. From the very beginning, he put a man and a woman in a garden and walked and talked with them. Ever since, people who know the Creator* have talked with him. And talking to God is called prayer.

Prayer has always been important to the people of God. In the Old Testament,* God spoke to Abraham* and gave him a promise. And Abraham built an altar* in that place and called on the name of the Lord.* Prayer was so important to the children of Abraham, that they offered prayers to God, just as Abraham did.

Many years after Abraham, his family went to Egypt* to find food. They stayed there for a long time because the leader of Egypt made them his slaves. Life was hard for them, so they cried out to God. And God answered their prayers and sent Moses* to bring them out of Egypt.

Part of the covenant,* the promises that God made with Abraham and Moses, told the people that they should pray. They should pray only to him and to no other God. Prayer was so important to them that the largest part of the Old Testament scriptures* is a book of songs and prayers. Many of the times that the children of Abraham worshipped, they used the words of these prayers to call on God and honor* him. Even Jesus grew up in a home where he would have known the prayers and heard them. He learned to pray as other children in Jewish homes did.

There are many ways that we may pray. We pray as we praise*
God for who he is and what he has done. We pray when we give
thanks to God. We admit that everything we have comes from
him, and without him we have no good thing. Since God sees our
hearts* as they really are, we pray when we confess. We speak to
God of things that we see in our lives that do not please him. We
pray when we ask him to meet the needs that we have. And we ask
him to meet the needs of other men and women.

We can pray at any time from wherever we are. And it does not
matter if we sit and pray, or stand and lift our hands to pray, or
bow with our face to the ground. God hears us when we pray.[1]

When we pray, we come to God knowing that we can come to
him only because of Jesus. We can talk to God only because Jesus
gave himself for us. That is why we should pray 'in Jesus' name.'
God wants us to come to him as a child who comes to a father. He
wants to give us good gifts, but he wants us to ask. God is pleased
when his children come to him.

We can pray at any time from wherever we are.

When we pray, we are to pray in the will of
God. And we are to pray with faith.* We do not
pray for what we know will not please God or
honor him. And we know what pleases and
honors God from what the scriptures tell us. If
we believe that our prayer is in God's will, then we must trust*
that he will answer our prayer.[2] The Holy Spirit will help us know
how to pray as we should. And when we do not know what to pray
for, the Holy Spirit* brings his own prayers to the Father for us.[3]

But if God already knows what we need, why should we pray?
We may not understand how prayer works. But we should pray
because our Father in heaven* tells us to pray. We should pray
because prayer is a way that we can be close to God. God has
decided to use our prayers as a part of his plans to change history.
God uses our prayers to do his work in the world. There are things
that happen because of prayer. And there are things that do not
happen because no one prayed.

Jesus told a story about a man who had a friend come to visit. But he had no food to feed his friend. So, the man went to his neighbor* and started to knock on his door. But it was midnight and the neighbor and his family were already in bed. But the man kept on knocking until his neighbor gave him what he wanted. Then Jesus said to his disciples* that they should pray like this man.[4] When they pray, they should not give up. If God does not answer, we should ask again. Sometimes, God asks us to wait. We may not always know why, but we do know that God has his reasons. God's answers always come at the right time.

1. 2 Samuel 7:18; Mark 11:25; 1 Chronicles 6:13; Daniel 6:10; Luke 22:41; Acts 7:60; Ephesians 3:14; Matthew 26:39; Mark 14:35; 1 Timothy 2:8

2. Matthew 21:22; Mark 11:24; James 1:6

3. Romans 8:26-27

4. Luke 11:5-10

121

What did Jesus* give us in order to teach us to pray?

Jesus gave us the Lord's* Prayer.

Matthew 6:9-15 • Luke 11:2-4

122

What is the Lord's Prayer?

Our Father in heaven,* may we give honor* to your name. May your Kingdom* come, may what you want to happen be done, on earth as it is in heaven. Give us today our daily bread. Forgive* us our sins,* just as we also have forgiven those who sin against us. Help us not to sin when we are tempted.* Protect us from the evil* one.

Matthew 6:9-13

123

How many requests are in the Lord's Prayer?

There are six requests.

We find the Lord's Prayer in two places in the Bible.* In Matthew,* Jesus teaches the prayer as he talks to a large group of people. In Luke,* Jesus teaches the prayer when he is with a smaller group of his disciples.* Jesus had been praying. One of his disciples said to him, 'John the Baptist* taught his disciples how to pray. Lord, teach us how to pray, too.'

So, Jesus gives them an example of how to pray. He tells them some of the things they ought to pray for. He tells them how to talk to their Father in heaven. Many Christians* learn this prayer by heart* so they can make the words a part of their prayers. Jesus does not tell them to pray this prayer word for word every time they pray. He says pray like this or pray in this way.

Jesus begins the prayer by saying, 'Our Father in heaven.' Any time we speak to God, it is good for us to remember who we are talking to. Jesus wants his disciples to remember that when they pray, they talk to God. He is the God who made the heavens. He is the God who is in heaven.

When we hear those words, 'in heaven,' it seems Jesus is saying that God is out there somewhere. Wherever it is, it is far away. But this phrase does not mean that God is far away. This phrase means the opposite of that. When Jesus says, 'our Father, who is in heaven,' he is telling them that God is near.

When the Jews* thought about heaven, they thought about three 'heavens.' They used the word to talk about the air, the sky, and the space around them. They also used the word 'heavens' to talk about the space above the clouds, the place of the sun, the moon, and stars. The Jews also used the word to talk about the heavens beyond the stars. Past time and space was the place where the angels* live. When Jesus says, 'our Father, in the heavens,' he is telling us that God is in all of those places. Yes, God is far away, but he is also near. He is close at hand. He is where we are. He is always where we can reach him.

In the Old Testament,* a woman named Hagar* was sent away from her family with her young son. She was alone with her son. They had no food. They lay under a tree and waited to die. But the scriptures* tell us that God heard the boy crying. And God called to Hagar from heaven and told her not to be afraid.[1]

God was where she was. He was there in the desert place. He was so close that he could hear a boy's cry. He was so close that he could whisper an answer to Hagar and she could hear him.

'Where can I go from your Spirit?* Where can I run from your presence?' David* asks. Then he says, 'If I rise to the heavens you are there. If I make my bed in the depths you are there.'[2]

When we pray 'Our Father in the heavens' we remind ourselves that God is not up there, out there, far away, but that God is near. God is close at hand. He is as real as the air that you just breathed. No matter where you are, God is there. God sees you. God hears you.

And Jesus says that God cares as a father cares for his children.[3] He loves us and wants to talk with us. The Jews almost never speak of God as Father. They used many names to honor* God when they prayed, but when they prayed to God, they did not call him Father. Abraham* is called a friend of God. He never calls God Father. Moses* speaks face to face with God and never calls God, Father. David fills the book of Psalms* with prayers, but he never prays to God as Father. But Jesus does it all the time. This had to be one of the things that the disciples noticed about Jesus' prayer that was different than any other prayers. These men had been praying their whole lives. But they had never prayed like this – like a child talking to a father. Perhaps that is why they wanted Jesus to teach them how to pray. So, Jesus begins his lesson by teaching them to call God, 'Father,' too.

---

1. Genesis 21:16-18
2. Psalm 139:7-12
3. Matthew 7:8-11; Luke 11:11-13

question 124

What is the first request?

'May we give honor* to your name.'

Matthew 6:9 • Luke 11:2

question 125

What do we pray for in the first request?

We pray that all people will praise* God's name.

Psalm 8:1-2 • Psalm 72:18-19 • Psalm 113:1-3

'May we honor your name' or 'may your name be kept holy.'*

That is the first thing Jesus* tells his disciples* to pray. When we say that God is holy, we say that God is perfect and set apart from everyone else. But what does it mean to keep his name holy?

Our names are important to us. When someone remembers our name, we feel pleased. When they use our name to speak well of us, we feel honored. People also use names to describe us. They give us a name that tells who we are or what we do. So, people may call us a brother or sister, a teacher or student, or a writer or a singer. Each of those names speak of a role that we have. It is a way for people to say who we are and how they see us.

We do not like it when people use our name to speak bad things about us. And we do not like it when people call us bad names. Our names are important to us. The scriptures* tell us that God's name is important to him as well. When God gave Moses* laws* for the people of Israel*, he said,

'You must not use the name of the Lord* your God in a bad or careless way.' And he said, 'Do not use my name as if it were not holy.'[1]

Our names say something about who we are and what we are like. So, the scriptures also use names for God to tell us who he is and what he is like. The Old Testament* writers call him, the Lord, Mighty and Strong; The God who made all things; the Lord, our peace;* and the Lord who provides. The Old Testament uses more than twenty names for the One, True God. When Jesus told his followers* to pray the words,

'May your name be kept holy,'

he had the Old Testament scriptures in mind. He wanted them to begin their prayers with praise. We praise God for who he is and what he has done. We thank him and honor him for all that he has done for us. And we ask that other people would honor him too.

So, Jesus wants us to remember who God is when we pray. He is mighty. He is strong. He provides. And he will not allow himself to be put to shame. So, we must speak of him in ways that honor him. And we must never give the honor that is due to him to anyone or anything else.[2]

We honor God's name when we speak of him with respect.* We believe that he is good, so we never speak of him as if he were not good.

We also bring honor to God's name when we obey him. Children can sometimes do things that are wrong. Sometimes, a child can bring shame upon their parents by the way they act. We can do the same thing when we do bad things. Or when we do not do what God tells us to do. When Israel did not follow God's laws, the nations near them thought less of Israel's God.[3] They caused the nations to say evil* things about him. The way that Israel could best honor God's name was to obey him.[4] So, it is important to 'set ourselves apart to be holy.'[5] The way to keep God's name holy is to be holy ourselves.

We honor God's name when we speak of him with respect.

When we follow God's commands, other people will notice. Jesus said that we are to do good so that people will see our good works and give honor to our Father in heaven.*[6] So, whether we eat or drink or do anything else, we are to do all that we do to give glory* to God.[7]

When we pray that God's name will be honored, we are also asking God to do great works and put his power on display. When God does mighty acts, people can see that he is holy and will give him glory. When God brought Israel out of Egypt,* he did many wonders there. He did that so the people would see his mighty works, know his great power, and honor his name.[8]

The first request teaches us to pray that God's people, wherever they are in the world, will act in a way that honors God. And we pray that we will be kept from doing things that would cause other men and women to think less of God and keep them from seeing who he is. We pray that all people would see the glory of God in us and in all of his people.

When we ask God to answer the first request, we can remind ourselves of God's promise. The day is coming when the whole world will see God for who he is. And the whole earth will know the glory of God's name.[9]

---

1. Exodus 20:7; Leviticus 22:31–32
2. Isaiah 48:9–11
3. Isaiah 52:5; Ezekiel 36:20–22; Romans 2:24
4. Leviticus 22:31–32, Ezekiel 39:7
5. Leviticus 20:7
6. Matthew 5:16
7. 1 Corinthians 10:31
8. Exodus 14:4; Exodus 14:17–18; Psalm 106:7–8
9. Isaiah 40:5

question ——
126

What is the second request?

'May your Kingdom* come.'

Matthew 6:10 • Luke 11:2

question ——
127

What do we pray for in the second request?

We pray that all people in the world will hear and believe the good news. We pray that they will obey Jesus* as Lord.*

John 17:20-21 • Acts 8:12 • Acts 28:30-31
Revelation 11:15

In the Scriptures,* the disciples* wrote about the kingdom.
Mark* and Luke* speak about the 'kingdom of God.' Matthew*
uses the phrase 'the kingdom of heaven.'* They seem to be
speaking of the same thing. The Gospels* tell us that Jesus talked
about the kingdom all the time.

But what did Jesus mean when he spoke of the kingdom?

This question is not easy to answer. One reason is that much
of what Jesus said about the kingdom, he said in parables.* A
parable is a short story that has a special meaning. Sometimes,
Jesus told these stories to help people understand what he talked
about. Sometimes, he used parables so that people would not
understand what he was saying.

Jesus said the kingdom of God is like a great wedding meal
because lots of people are invited to come. The kingdom of God
is like something of great value that is hidden in a field. The
kingdom of heaven is like a man who owns land. He hires people
to work in his field. Some start work at the beginning of the day,
some in the middle of the day, and some at the end of the day. But
when the work day is over he pays them all the same amount. He
said the kingdom of God is like a small seed. It is very small, but
it grows very big.[1]

He also said things about the kingdom as he walked with his
disciples. He said that it is easier for a camel to go through the
eye of a needle than it is for a rich man to enter the kingdom. He
says that if you want to enter the kingdom you have to do so like a
little child. He said that you should look for the kingdom of God
and what is right before you look for anything else. When you do,
everything else in this world – like food and clothing – will be
added to them.

So how do we understand 'may your kingdom come?'

A kingdom is where someone has authority. We may not have a king where we live. But we do understand what having a king means. A kingdom is the place where the king is the boss. In that place, the king's word is law.* The kingdom of God is found where God is king.

The Old Testament* tells us that God rules over all things. He is the Lord most high, a great king over all the earth.[2] And the New Testament* says that Jesus came to earth to establish a kingdom.

When we believe in Jesus, we become a part of his kingdom. This kingdom began with a small group of people. But it has been growing. And now, in every part of the world, there are men and women who know and follow Jesus, their king. If Jesus rules in someone's life, the kingdom of heaven is there. If Jesus rules in someone's home, the kingdom of heaven is there.

But Jesus and the prophets* and apostles* also spoke about the kingdom in another way. They spoke of a day when God's kingdom will be complete. All who are a part of this kingdom will know God and honor* him. In every place and in every heart,* Jesus will rule. And the kingdom will cover the whole earth 'as the waters cover the sea.'[3] When Christ returns, he will set up his kingdom and bring heaven to earth. He will make a new heaven and a new earth. He will live there with his people forever and ever.

When we pray 'may your kingdom come,' we are praying for the kingdom of God to come to earth where Jesus Christ will rule forever and ever. But we are also praying that the kingdom would be here and now. And that it would grow and grow. We pray that people would hear the good news of the kingdom and obey the king now. When people believe and obey the gospel, they are part of the Body of Christ on earth. They belong in the new kingdom.

We ask God to help us live today as we will one day live. As citizens of the kingdom, we are to begin to live in a way that honors our King. We obey our king. What Jesus says is our law. And we are to become the hands and the heart, the feet and the ears, and the welcoming arms of Jesus.

How does this kingdom come? We take the good news of Jesus to every land and people. When people come to believe, they become part of the kingdom. They become people who honor Jesus as King of kings and Lord of lords. And they will be among those who will live in the new heaven and new earth that he will make when he comes back.

When we pray, 'may your kingdom come,' we ask God to complete the promise that he made to Abraham* and David.* We pray that he will do everything in us and on the earth that the prophets said he would do. We pray that he will return and fix all of the things that are broken. We pray for the day when every knee will bow before the Lord Jesus. When we pray, 'may your kingdom come,' we pray that this day will come soon.

---

1. Matthew 13:44; Matthew 20:1-16;   2. Psalm 4:1-4   4. Habakkuk 2:14
   Mark 4:30-34; Matthew 13:47-52   3. Psalm 74:12

question — 128

What is the third request?

'May what you want to happen be done on earth as it is in heaven.'*

Matthew 6:10

question — 129

What do we pray for in the third request?

We pray that people on earth will do as God desires in every way, just like the angels* do in heaven.

Psalm 103:19-22 • Psalm 143:10

The scriptures* speak of God's will in several ways. In some places, God's will is what God has decided will happen. This part of God's will is mostly hidden from us. We do not know what God has in mind until after it happens. The story of Joseph* in the Old Testament* is an example of this.

His brothers sold Joseph as a slave. He was taken to Egypt.* A woman lied about him, so he went to prison. Later, he would tell the leader in Egypt what the leader's dream meant. Then, he would help his family and give them food when they had no food. And he would become a powerful leader in Egypt. At first, neither his brothers nor Joseph knew that God was at work in all of these things. But later, Joseph understood that all of the things that happened to him were part of God's will.[1]

Paul* spoke of God as the one 'who works all things in a way that fits his plan and purpose.'[2] Paul may have been thinking of what God said through the prophet* Isaiah.* 'What I plan will come to pass. I will do everything that I desire to do.'[3] There are times when the scriptures show that God causes something to happen. There are times when he allows things to happen that do not please him. But even in those things, God is working his good purposes.

The scripture also speaks of God's will as the things that God has revealed to us in the Bible.* So, God's will is what God wants us to do (and not do). We may not understand all that God is doing in the world. But he has not hidden what he wants us to do. God has made those things clear in the scriptures. So, we find God's commands to us all through the Bible. God wants us to be kind to one another. Love our neighbors.* Do not steal. Do not get drunk. And act justly,* love mercy,* and walk humbly before our God.[4]

We also ask God to help us to obey his will when it is clear to us. God has shown us what he wants us to do. He has shown us the kind of people he wants us to be. So, we pray that God would help us to do what we know that we should do. And to do these things as quickly as the angels in heaven. But we cannot do God's will this way unless we put aside our own will. That does not mean that we put away all of our desires. But when we find in ourselves desires that would not please our Father in heaven, we deny our desires to follow his.[5]

When we pray, 'may your will be done,' we must remember both of the ways God's will is used. We submit* to God's purposes for us each day. We do not always know what will happen in our life each day. But when we pray, 'may what you want to happen be done' we remind ourselves that God has a purpose for all that happens. We pray this way so that we can be ready to accept whatever God sends or does not send.

When we pray this prayer, we are like a man who has a guest come to his home. The man welcomes his friend and says, 'Please make yourself at home.' Then, he hands his friend the keys to his house. He may expect that his friend may want to change some things in his house. But because he trusts his friend, he believes that whatever the friend does will be for good. When we pray this way, we give God the key to our lives. We tell him to come in and do as he pleases. We are handing the control of our 'kingdom'* to Jesus, our King.

This part of the prayer should also give us hope.* God's will is being done today in heaven. Now we are asking the God who rules the heavens to do his will in our lives, this day and every day. So, this request helps us to look for ways to be a part of what God desires to do on earth.

When we pray, 'may Your will be done,' we are asking God to help us to desire the same things that he desires. When we come to want what he wants, we find true joy no matter what a day may bring. And this is the work that the Holy Spirit* is doing in us. He helps us to know God's will. He helps us to trust* that God's ways are best. The God, who is good, is in control of our lives. When we pray, 'may your will be done,' it is the best thing that we can ask for.

When I pray the Lord's* Prayer, I am asking to be a part of God's good purposes. I connect with the God who is Father. And I submit to the Father who is King.

———

ACT JUSTLY, LOVE MERCY, AND WALK HUMBLY BEFORE OUR GOD.

———

1. Genesis 37-50
2. Ephesians 1:11
3. Isaiah 46:10

4. Micah 6:8; Ephesians 4:32;
   Matthew 5:43-48; Ephesians 5:28

5. Matthew 16:24;
   Matthew 26:39-44; John 5:30;
   John 6:38; John 13:1-17

question — 130

What is the fourth request?

'Give us today our daily bread.'

Matthew 6:11 • Luke 11:3

question — 131

What do we pray for in the fourth request?

We pray that God will give us all things that we need for our bodies.

Psalm 145:15-16 • Proverbs 30:8-9 • Matthew 6:31-33

The first three requests in the Lord's* Prayer are about God. We are to honor* God's name, wait for God's kingdom,* and submit* to God's will. These are the things that Jesus* wants us to pray about first. With the fourth request, we turn to God and ask that he provide for our daily needs. Asking God for something is the most basic idea of prayer. Prayer is more than that, but it is not less. These are the first words in the Lord's Prayer where Jesus taught us to ask for something for ourselves.

God's people have always known that all that we have is a gift from him. That God owns all things and all good things come from him.[1] Jesus wants us to remember that each time we pray.

Jesus says that we should ask for bread because bread is our most basic need. He wants us to pray about the most basic things that are on our mind, so he uses bread. Bread is not a big thing. Bread was the most basic food in Jesus' day. But if you do not have it, you think about it a lot. We cannot live very long without food.

He used bread as a way to speak about all of our needs. When Jesus tells us to pray for bread, he is telling us to pray for bread and everything else as well. We need to grow the grain to make bread. So, we pray for rain and sun so that our fields will grow. We need to work to have money to buy bread. And we cannot work if we are sick, so we pray that our body will be healthy. Jesus wants us to see the word 'bread' to remind us of all of these things.

When Jesus says, 'daily bread' it seems that he wants us to pray this way every day. When the people in Jesus' day heard this word, they would hear, 'enough for today.' The masters in those days paid workers at the end of each day. They would use the money they made that day to buy the food for that day. So, Jesus wants people to remember to ask God to give them what they need- 'enough for today.'

In the book of Matthew,* Jesus tells people not to worry about clothes or food. God knows that we need these things. Instead, they are to 'first seek the kingdom of God and what he says is right.'² When they do, God will provide them with what they need. God is a good Father. He knows how to give good gifts to his children.³

Later, Paul* would tell the Philippians*, 'God will supply all of your needs.'⁴ When we pray this prayer, we are telling God that we are depending on him to do that.

In this request, we do not ask for all the things we want or wish we had. We trust* God to give us what we really need. This prayer does not teach us that we should not work. Work is the way God provides our needs. When God put Adam* and Eve* in the garden, he gave them work to do.⁵

Jesus also wants us to care for those in need. He uses two words here that he has not used before. Give us, this day, our daily bread. This is not just a prayer for each person to ask for things for themselves. When we pray this prayer, we pray as a member of a family. We pray as part of a community.* So, when God gives us more than we need, we must think of those who do not have enough. We are to depend on God. And we are to remember that other men and women may be depending on us. When God gives us much more than we need, we are to think about those who may not have enough.⁶

GOD WILL SUPPLY ALL OF YOUR NEEDS.

God may use us to be the answer to someone else's prayers. We can give people their daily bread if we have enough. We must not say no to helping other men and women in need. It is wrong to be selfish with our money. Mark tells us about a poor widow who only had two small coins. She was poor, but she trusted God and gave them away to help other men and women. Jesus was pleased with her.[7]

When we pray this prayer, we ask God to provide just what we need. We ask for what we need, when we need it – forevery area of life.

1. 1 Chronicles 29:13-14; Psalm 24:1; Romans 11:36
2. Matthew 6:33
3. Matthew 7:11-12; Luke 11:10-14
4. Philippians 4:19
5. Genesis 1:25-29; Genesis 2:15
6. Deuteronomy 15:7-8
7. Mark 12:41-44

question — 132

What is the fifth request?

'Forgive* us our sins,* just as we also have forgiven those who sin against us.'

Matthew 6:12 • Luke 11:4

question — 133

What do we pray for in the fifth request?

We pray that God will forgive our sins. And we pray that God will help us to forgive those who have hurt us.

Psalm 51:2-3 • Matthew 5:23-24 • Ephesians 4:32

Christians* say this part of the Lord's* Prayer in different ways in different parts of the world. Some say the prayer with the word 'sins.' Some use the word 'trespasses.' Some say 'debts.' That is because the Scripture* speaks of sin in many ways. Sin is breaking the law. Sin is falling short of what God wants for us. Sin is fighting against God. Sin is being unclean. The word 'trespass' is a word that says that someone is in a place where they should not be. For example, we see a wall, and on the wall is a sign that says,

'Do Not Enter.'

If we climb the wall and go into that place, we trespass. We enter when we have no right to be there. When we sin, we go outside the law* of God. We enter a place where we should not be.

In the book of Matthew,* Jesus* says that sin is like a debt that has not been paid. Matthew was writing to readers who were Jews.* Many Jews talked about sin this way. When we sin, we owe a debt, and we must pay with our lives. We deserve death. We owed a debt that we could not pay. But Jesus paid our debt for us. He died so that we would not have to die.[1]

This prayer asks God to 'forgive us our sins.' The word 'forgive' means to let go. If you are holding something in a cage and you open the door, you let it go. In the Lord's Prayer, it means to let go of the debt that someone owes to you. You let them go without a demand that they be punished. God has every right to demand payment and punish us. But in this request, we ask him not to. We ask him to let us go. We ask for mercy.*

Sometimes, Jesus speaks of God as a judge. Here in Matthew, Jesus speaks of God as a Father. Because of what Jesus did for us, we will not be judged for our sin and put away from God. Instead, God welcomes us into his family. But as children in his family, we want to please our Father.[2] So, we do those things that honor* him. God is pleased with us when we forgive other people who have done bad things to us.

This request shows us that the way that we forgive other men and women is connected to the way God has forgiven us. We should be people who forgive because we have been forgiven. If we do not forgive, it is a sign that we do not understand how much God has forgiven us. If we do not want to make a sacrifice* to forgive other men and women, we do not understand how much Jesus sacrificed for us.

We forgive people that do wrong. That does not mean that we let them hurt us. It does not mean that we do not speak to them about what they have done. It does not mean that we do not get help from other men and women to get them to stop. It does mean that we do not hold anger in our hearts* against them. Even if they are our enemies, we are not unkind to them or try to hurt them because they have hurt us.

> Peter* came to Jesus and asked, 'Lord, how many times may my brother sin against me and I forgive him, up to seven times?' Jesus said to him, 'I tell you, not seven times but seventy times seven.'[3]

And that is why we have to pray this prayer again, and again, and again. Because sometimes it takes time to find the grace* to forgive the person who has hurt you. This prayer reminds us that God has forgiven us foreverything. He has taken away our debt. He has let us go free. Since that is true, how can we do any less for all those people who have hurt us?

Each time we pray this prayer, we are to remember to thank God that he has forgiven us. And we are to ask for the help of the Holy Spirit* to forgive those whom we need to forgive.

And that is the reason those two phrases are joined together in this prayer. It does not mean that God will only forgive me if I forgive other people. That is not how grace works. But it does mean that when I know that God has forgiven me, I will be a person who forgives.

1. Matthew 20:28; Romans 5:8; Romans 5:10; 1 Corinthians 15:3; 1 Peter 3:18

2. Matthew 6:1-18; Luke 5:16
3. Matthew 18:21-22; Romans 12:14-21

134

What is the sixth request?

Help us not to sin* when we are tempted.* Protect us from the evil* one.

Matthew 6:13 • Luke 11:4

135

What do we pray for in the sixth request?

We pray that God will keep us from sin. And protect us from evil.

Psalm 119:11 • 1 Corinthians 10:13 • 2 Timothy 4:18

This part of the Lord's* Prayer reminds us that our world is a broken place. Things go wrong that can make trouble for us. These troubles can sometimes come from the outside of us. We can become sick. People may decide to hurt us or do things to make our lives difficult. Storms and floods and fires are a part of the world that we live in. This request reminds us that followers* of Jesus* have the same kinds of problems that other people have. Sometimes, their problems can be even greater. Jesus said that, if we follow him, the world could hate us just as it hated him.

When we pray this way, we can see that we must be delivered from sin or trouble or the Evil One.* When we read the Psalms,* many of the songs of Israel* were songs asking God to deliver them from their enemies. Some Psalms asked God to deliver them from people who were hurting them.[1] Other songs called on God to deliver them from their own sinful desires and ways.[2]

But, sometimes, God allows us to go through hard times. James* tells us that God will not tempt us to sin. But God allows us to go through trials that test us. He is at work to make us more like Jesus. One of the tools he uses to do this is to allow us to go through difficulty. His purpose is to make us stronger.[3]

We ask that God spare us from being tempted to sin because Satan,* the Evil One, tries to use each test to hurt us. Satan is our enemy. He will always use any way that he can to get us to doubt God or to sin. And we pray to avoid being tempted because sometimes these difficulties cause us great pain.

We pray 'Lead us not into temptation'* because we know our own weaknesses. We know that trials can cause us to be tempted to act in bad ways. Even blessings,* if we forget where they come from, can become a temptation to sin. We can become proud and forget our need for God when everything is good. So, both good and bad things can become tests for us. The Evil One has great skill, and we are weak.

268 | PRAYER AND HOPE

In many ways, God's work in us is a mystery. We know that he wants us to be holy* and know his joy. But we also see in the scripture* that God does not always keep us from being tested. He allows those tests to help us grow. But God will be with us through the test. And he will help us to resist when the Evil One tempts us to sin.[4]

We must always be aware that bad things can happen in our lives. But we know that God is in control of even these things. He has either sent them or allows them, to test us and make us strong. But when these tests come, we can trust* that God has the power to deliver us from the evil they bring. And God can keep us from falling as we go through the trials life brings to us.[5]

God has forgiven* us and welcomed us into his family. He is making us more and more like Jesus. But, until Jesus returns, we still have the evil desires that fight against us and that we are to fight against. Sin in our hearts* causes us to want to do things that are not what God wants for us. We still find in us desires to love someone or something more than God himself. We pray that God would provide the strength and the wisdom to do what is right and best. And when we find that we have overcome the temptation and been loyal to God, we thank him for delivering us.

Jesus never asks us to act as if there is no evil in the world. But he tells his disciples* that God is doing something about it. He can bring good out of it. And one day, God will remove evil from the world.[6] But while we wait, we trust him to give us the strength to refuse the Evil One. And to stand up under the trials we face. That is why we are to make this request. And each time he helps us through a trial, we thank him for his mercy* and we give him the glory* that is due him.

---

1. Psalm 13; Psalm 35; Psalm 143   3. James 1:2-12   5. Jude 24
2. Psalm 36; Psalm 51   4. 1 Corinthians 10:3   6. Revelation 21:1-4

What does prayer teach us?

Prayer teaches us that we must trust* God completely for his help.

Ephesians 6:18 • Philippians 4:6 • Hebrews 4:16

For many years and in many places, Christians* have used the words of the Lord's* Prayer to help them pray. In some places, people add a short sentence at the end of the prayer. 'For yours is the kingdom* and the power and the glory* forever and ever. Amen.'* Jesus did not say these words, but they do seem to fit many of the other things Jesus said.

People use the word 'doxology'* to describe a phrase like this. A doxology is a psalm* or words of praise* that people use to honor* God. When Christians end their prayer this way, they are saying that God is King.[1] And he will be King forever and ever. As King, he has power to do all that he has promised.[2] And when he sets up his kingdom on this earth (and he will), all people will see his glory and honor him.

THE LORD'S PRAYER TEACHES US HOW TO PRAY.

To pray this way helps us to remember why we know that God can be trusted. God knows all things, so he cannot be surprised. God has all power and no one and no thing, can stand against him and succeed. And God is good. He is a God of grace* and acts with kindness to his people. He is able to make all things work together in a way that moves his purposes forward. That is why we pray. That is why we should praise.

So, many Christians end the prayer as it began, with praise. Although prayer and praise are not the same thing, they go together. The more we know God, the more we trust him. The more we trust him, the more we pray. The more we pray, the more we will see our good God at work as he answers our prayers. The more we see God at work, the more reasons we have to praise him.

Remember that his disciples* asked Jesus* to teach them how to pray because they saw how much he prayed.[3] Some watched him as he prayed at his baptism.* They saw him rise early from sleep to pray. He prayed for the children as he blessed* them. He prayed before he healed people and after he healed people. Before he chose the twelve men who would follow him, he prayed all night. He prayed when he sent them out and prayed when they returned. They heard Jesus pray. And they saw God answer his prayers.

Jesus prayed because he loved the Father. But he also prayed to be an example to his followers. He prayed to show them how to worship the Father. He prayed to show them how to submit to the Father and depend on him. And he prayed so that they would know that the Father had sent him.[4]

Paul* says that, like Jesus, we should pray all of the time. We should talk to God about everything. We should pray all kinds of prayers. And we should always keep on praying.[6] When we do, Paul says that we will receive mercy.* We will find grace whenever we need help.[7]

God has an eternal* plan. He does many things to complete that plan. He does many of those things through our prayers. God does some things when we pray. And some things he will not do unless we pray.

So, the Lord's Prayer teaches us how to pray. We are to give God praise. We are to confess* how we need him to keep us from sin.* We thank him for all that he has done. And we ask him to meet all of our needs and the needs of other people too. He knows how to give good gifts to his children, and he will give them when we ask.[8]

It takes only one minute to say the Lord's Prayer. But in that short time, it teaches us lessons that can guide us for the rest of our lives. God is our Father and is no longer our judge. The world is not what it is supposed to be. But God's kingdom will soon make all things new. God owns all things and gives us everything that we need. God offers to forgive,* even when we do not deserve it and have done nothing to earn it. When God forgives us of our sins, he helps us to forgive other men and women when they do wrong things to us. Life is hard. Bad things sometimes happen. But God will keep us and deliver us when we trust him.

1. Psalm 103:19
2. Psalm 47; Psalm 93; Psalm 97; Psalm 145
3. Luke 11:1

4. Romans 11:33–36; Ephesians 3:20; 1 Timothy 6:13–16; Hebrews 13:20; Revelation 1:4–7
5. Hebrews 2:17; Jude 24–25

6. 1 Thessalonians 5:17
7. Ephesians 6:18; Philippians 4:6; Hebrews 4:16
8. Matthew 7:8–11; Luke 11:9–13

question — 137

Where is Christ* now?

Christ is now in heaven* at the right side of God the Father.

Mark 16:19 • Acts 5:31 • Romans 8:34

question — 138

Will Christ come to the earth again?

Yes. He will come to be the judge of all the people in the world at the last day. And he will save those who are waiting for him.

Matthew 25:31-32 • 2 Thessalonians 1:7-9
2 Timothy 4:1 • Hebrews 9:28

After Jesus* rose from death, more than 500 hundred people saw him. He appeared to all of the disciples* and spent time with them. He taught them many things from the Old Testament* that they had not understood before. He also told them to go into all the world and tell the gospel* story to everyone.[1]

After 40 days, he went with some of his disciples out of town. While they were talking, Jesus began to go up into the sky. The word 'ascend' means to go up. So, Christians call the time when Jesus went up to return to his Father in heaven, the Ascension. While the disciples watched, he went into a cloud. He continued up into the sky until they could no longer see him.

Jesus had told his disciples that he would soon return to his Father. That is what happened.

While they were looking up into the sky, two men appeared to them. These men had on white clothing. They were angels.* They asked them, 'Why are you looking into heaven? This same Jesus who was taken up from you into heaven, will come again in this same way.'[2] But until that day comes, Jesus will be with the Father in heaven.

The New Testament* tells us some things about what Jesus is now doing in heaven. Sometimes, the scriptures* say, Jesus is in heaven, standing, ready to take action.[3] Sometimes, he is walking among his people there.[4] But the New Testament most often says that Jesus sits at the Father's right hand.[5] He does not sit by his Father to rest. He sits there to rule. The right side of the Father is a place of authority.

The scripture also says that Jesus is Lord* of all. And because of what he did on the cross,* God the Father has given him a name above every name. He has given Jesus the right to rule all of heaven and earth.[6]

Jesus is also at the Father's side to act as our mediator.* A mediator is a go-between. A mediator stands between two people or nations that are at war. And he brings them together to find peace.* So Jesus speaks to the Father for us to bring peace between us.

The scriptures tell us that we were God's enemies. We had turned against God and refused to obey his law.* So, because we had done these things, God was going to judge us and punish us for what we had done. But God the Father sent his Son to be our Mediator instead.[7]

> **Jesus speaks to the Father for us to bring peace between us.**

Jesus came to be one of us. He did all that the Father asked of him. He obeyed God's law in every way. Then he went to the cross. He died there to take the punishment that we deserve. He died so that we did not have to. Now, he is at the Father's side and speaks to the Father for us.

Once Jesus sat down at the right hand of God the Father, the Father, then, sent the Holy Spirit* to us.[8] He sent the Holy Spirit to work in us and through us. And the Father sent the Holy Spirit to help us to bring honor* to himself and the Son.

Paul* teaches that, some day, Jesus will return to earth from the sky. He will come in a physical body.[9] There will be trumpets playing loudly. An angel will make a loud shout. The believers* who have already died and been buried will come alive again. And they will join Jesus in the air. Then the believers who are still alive on the earth will be taken up into the air also.[10] They will join Jesus in the air. Then, with them, Jesus will return to the earth. He will raise the dead and he will judge all of the men and women who have ever lived.[11] He will welcome those who have trusted him. He will punish those who did not. Jesus will bring an end to this world as it is now. And will make all things new.[12]

---

1. Mark 16:15
2. Acts 1:9-11
3. Acts 7:56; Revelation 1:1-16; Revelation 14:1
4. Revelation 2:1
5. Ephesians 3:20; 1 Peter 3:22
6. Matthew 28:18-20; Philippians 2:9; Colossians 2:10
7. 1 Timothy 2:5; Hebrews 8:6; Hebrews 9:15
8. John 14:16; John 14:26; John 15:26; John 16:7
9. Matthew 24:44; Acts 1:11; Colossians 3:4; 2 Timothy 4:8; Hebrews 9:28
10. 1 Thessalonians 4:16-17
11. Matthew 25:31; Acts 17:31; Romans 2:16; 2 Corinthians 5:10
12. Matthew 19:28; Romans 8:19-21; 2 Peter 3:10-13; Revelation 21:5

question —

139

What happens to the righteous* at death?

The bodies of the righteous return to the dust. Their souls* go to be with the Lord.*

Genesis 3:19 • Ecclesiastes 12:7 • 2 Corinthians 5:8

question —

140

What happens to wicked people at death?

The bodies of the wicked return to dust. Their souls suffer punishment. God keeps them for the day when he comes to judge.

Luke 16:23-24 • John 5:28-29 • 2 Peter 2:9

All people have a body and a soul. God made both the soul and the body, so both the body and the soul are good. But the body and soul are not eternal* like God is. They only live as long as God decides to give them life. A body may die. But the scriptures* tell us that God will cause the soul to live somewhere forever. The Bible* is clear that death is not the end for anyone.[1]

When the body dies, the soul leaves the body. A body can die and be buried. But the soul continues to live. The soul continues as it was before the body died.

The scriptures say that the souls of both the righteous and the wicked go to a place to wait. They both wait for their bodies to be raised to life again. But the righteous and the wicked do not go to the same place. And they do not experience the same things.

One story in the scriptures speaks of the soul after death. Two men died. One was poor and the other was rich. But, after they died, the souls of both men were still alive. Both men had gone to a place that was different than where they had been with their bodies. Both men knew who they were. They knew other people who were with them. They remembered what they had done in the past. Their souls continued after their bodies had died. The poor man found rest and comfort where he was. The rich man found no rest or comfort. He went to a place of terrible suffering with no one there to show him mercy.*[2] Jesus used the word 'hell'*[3] to speak of the place where the rich man went. There was only sorrow where he was, but he could not get out of that place.

When righteous people die, they go to a place of rest and comfort. The righteous are those who have been made right with God. They believe that Jesus is the son of God and they have trusted him to save them. For the righteous, death is to be 'away from the body and at home with the Lord.'[4] When a believer* dies, their body goes to the grave. But their soul goes to be with Christ the

> ## For the righteous, death is to be 'away from the body and at home with the Lord.'

moment that their body dies. There, they wait for the day when they will return to the earth and enjoy a new life in a new body. Paul* tells of this time when the bodies of believers will be raised to life again many places in the New Testament.*[5]

The scriptures say that the souls of all who have died and are right with God are in heaven.* There, they have been made perfect.[6] We do not know everything about what heaven will be like. But we do know that it will be 'far better' than what we are doing here.[7]

For those who do not trust* Jesus, their souls are taken to a holding place as soon as their body dies. In this place, there is no rest or comfort. They wait there until the day God will bring the souls of all people to return to their bodies again. All people will be raised from the dead. Then, they will be alive again, body and soul, to stand before God. They will stand before God, in their new bodies, to be judged. God will judge them and send them to a place that is much worse than where they were before. And they will be there forever and ever.

After death, no one can change from evil to righteous. After death, all that remains for those who are evil is judgement.*[8]

---

1. John 3:16-18; Hebrews 9:27
2. Luke 16:19-31
3. Matthew 5:29-30; Matthew 10:28; Matthew 18:9; Matthew 23:33; Luke 12:5; Luke 16:23
4. 2 Corinthians 5:6-8
5. 1 Corinthians 15:50-54; 1 Thessalonians 4:13-17
6. Hebrews 12:22-23
7. Philippians 1:23
8. Revelation 20:14-15

question 141

Will the dead be raised to life again?

Yes, all the dead shall be raised when Christ* comes again.

Daniel 12:2 • John 5:28-29 • Acts 24:14-15

question 142

What will happen to the wicked people in the day Christ comes to judge?

God will punish them in hell* with a destruction that never ends. They will be cast out from God's presence forever.

Matthew 25:41,46 • Mark 9:47-48 • Luke 12:5
Luke 16:23-26 • 2 Thessalonians 1:9
Revelation 20:12-15

question 143

What will happen to the righteous* people?

The righteous people will live happily with God. They will live forever in a new heaven* and a new earth.

Isaiah 66:22-23 • 2 Peter 3:13 • Revelation 21:2-4

Jesus* rose from the dead and then went up into heaven in his new body.[1] When Jesus returns to the earth, he will come in the same body that he had when he went away.[2] When he returns, he will come to raise the dead and to judge the world.[3]

After Jesus raises all people to life again, everyone will give an account of themselves to God. Jesus will judge all people.[4] And God, through Christ, will reward or punish people for what they have done.[5] Because Jesus knows all things and is holy,* he is the perfect judge. No one can hide the truth from him. No one can trick him or lie to him.

All those who have trusted in Jesus and have died will receive a new body that will be like his body. Those who have trusted in Christ and are still alive when he comes will receive a new body too.[6] That body will be like the body we have now, but it will also be different in many ways. This new body will not grow old. It will not become sick. It will be a perfect body that will live forever. Paul* calls it a glorified body.[7] A glorified body is one in which there is no sin.* And it is a body that cannot die. But even with new bodies, believers will be able to know other people as we know other people now. They will see friends and family who have died before them, and they will know each other.[8] People who have been apart for a long time will be together again. Those who have trusted Jesus will also be given a new home. This new home is called heaven.

Heaven is the place that Christ has been preparing for those who have believed and trusted in him.[9] It is a place of rest. In heaven there will be constant joy. The believers* will worship* and praise* God and Christ.[10] They will experience Christ's love for them in a way that they could never understand before.[11] There will be fellowship with Christ and with other believers. And it will never end.[12]

The people who have not trusted in Jesus will also go to a new home. But this new home is not like heaven. Hell is a place where people will suffer. This suffering will last forever in a place of fire and darkness.[13] It is a place of weeping and misery.[14] It is a place of destruction. Smoke from the fire there will go up forever. Those who go there have chosen the path that took them there. They loved darkness instead of light. They have not loved their Creator* as their Lord.* They did not accept Jesus and refused to come to him.[15] Because of these things, they will be punished. They will have no rest day or night. There are no chances to escape. They cannot go back and change anything that they have done in the past.

At the judgement,* people will know that Jesus is just and what he says is right.[16] God knows the hearts* and minds of all people. God is fair. He does what is right and good. When Jesus comes again, no one who has trusted in Jesus will suffer at his hand.

1. Acts 26:23
2. Matthew 24:44; Acts 1:11; Colossians 3:4; 1 Thessalonians 5:1-4; 2 Timothy 4:8; Hebrews 9:28
3. John 5:28-29
4. Matthew 13:40-43; Matthew 25:41-46; John 5:22-30; Acts 10:42; 2 Corinthians 5:10; 2 Timothy 4:1; Hebrews 9:27; Hebrews 10:25-31; Hebrews 12:23; 2 Peter 3:7; Jude 6-7; Revelation 20:10-15
5. Matthew 16:27; Romans 2:6; 2 Corinthians 5:10; Revelation 22:12
6. 1 Corinthians 15:50-54; 2 Corinthians 5:1-5
7. 1 Corinthians 15:45-54
8. 1 Thessalonians 4:13-18
9. John 14:1-3
10. Hebrews 12:22-25; Revelation 7:9-10; Revelation 19:1-5
11. Matthew 25:34; Ephesians 3:17-19; 1 Peter 1:3-9; Revelation 7:17
12. Revelation 19:6-9; Revelation 22:5
13. Jude 7; Jude 13
14. Matthew 8:12; Matthew 13:42; Matthew 22:13; Matthew 24:51; Matthew 25:30; Luke 16:23; Revelation 20:10; 2 Thessalonians 1:7-9; 1 Thessalonians 5:3; 2 Peter 3:7
15. John 3:18-21; Romans 1:18-32; Romans 2:8; 2 Thessalonians 2:9-11
16. Genesis 18:25; Deuteronomy 32:4; Job 8:4

question ———

144

What will the new heaven* and the new earth be like?

In the new heaven and the new earth we will be with God. We will never sin.* We will never die. There will be no more curse.* There will be no more sadness and no more pain. We will never be guilty, afraid or ashamed. We will know the joy that comes from God.

Hebrews 12:22-23 • Jude 24 • Revelation 21:1-5
Revelation 22:1-4

The scripture* tells us that after Jesus returns, heaven and earth will pass away.[1] Then, the Lord* Jesus* will make everything new.[2] He will replace heaven and earth with a new heaven and a new earth. Isaiah* says that the new heaven and new earth will go on and on and the people there will be full of joy. Peter* says that only what is right and good will be there.[3]

In this new place, God will build a great city. John* calls it 'the Holy* City,' the New Jerusalem* that comes down out of heaven from God. God the Father, Jesus the Lamb,* and the Holy Spirit* will live there.[4] The city will have streets and gates, and they will be beautiful and strong. And there will be angels* at each of the gates.

The people that Jesus has rescued will fill the city.[5] There will be so many people that no one can tell how many there are. There will be people there from every nation and every family and every language. And they will all sing and give thanks to God.

Those who have trusted Jesus will live in this new heaven and new earth forever. We will have new bodies that are like Jesus' body after he rose from death. In those bodies we will be able to see and feel and enjoy all of the things God has made for us there. The tree of life will grow in the new city and we can eat from it. And we can drink from a river there that will be as clear as glass.[6]

In heaven, we will worship God. We will enjoy all of the other people who are there. And we will have work to do. Work that will please God and will please us.

We know the most about the new heaven and earth from John. God let John see the new city and he wrote about it in the book of Revelation.* What John remembered most about that place was what was not there. In the new heaven and earth, no one will ever be sick, and no one will ever suffer. No one will ever die because there is no death there. No one will weep or be sad ever again, for God will wipe away every tear from our eyes.

The curse that God put upon the earth will be gone and the world will be just like God made it to be. There will be no broken things there.[7] All sin will be gone and no evil* can ever enter there. And we will no longer have any desire to do wrong. Our hearts* will be clean and we will be able to love God with all of our heart and mind and strength. We will never feel fear or shame or guilt.* We will be like Jesus and we will see him as he is.[8]

Although this new heaven and new earth will not come until Jesus returns, we are already citizens of this New Jerusalem. And some day, we will live in this most perfect place God has promised to us. Then, God will make his home with us. We will be his people. And God himself will be with us and be our God. And we will see his face.[9]

The new heavens and new earth are the end of the story God tells us in the Bible.* Jesus does all that he promised to do. He has put all of his enemies under his feet. And Jesus will fix everything that was broken. He will put the world back to be what God made it to be in the beginning. He will have kept all of the promises that he made to Abraham* and to David.* But the new heaven and the new earth are not the end of the story. It is the beginning of a new story, a story that will go on and on forever.

---

1. Mark 13:31
2. Revelation 21:5
3. Isaiah 65:17; Isaiah 66:22;
   2 Peter 3:13

4. Revelation 21:22
5. Revelation 22:3
6. Revelation 22:1-3

7. Revelation 21:1-4;
   Revelation 21:3-5
8. 1 John 3:2
9. Revelation 22:1-4

The *Story* *of* Jesus

When you read this book, it does not take long before you begin to notice something. Jesus* is very important to the men and women who worked on it. There are many reasons for that. For example, many people say that Jesus was a prophet.* They say that Jesus spoke for God. We believe that too. But we believe that Jesus was much more than a prophet.

Other people say that Jesus was a wise man, a teacher. And during his life, Jesus taught many true and helpful things. We believe that too. But we believe that Jesus was much more than a wise teacher.

Some people say that Jesus was a good example to follow. He lived the kind of life that all people should try to live. We believe that too. If we all lived as Jesus did, we would be better people. The world would be a better place. But we believe that Jesus was much more than a good example.

So, What Do We Believe About Jesus?

We believe that Jesus is God; God who became a man to rescue the world. In fact, the story of the Bible* is the story of God's plan to rescue the world through his Son, Jesus. One of the men who wrote about Jesus said it this way:

God loved the world so much that he gave his only Son, Jesus. God did this so that whoever puts his trust* in Jesus will not be lost, but will have life that lasts forever.

But if you have never heard anyone speak about Jesus in this way, you may have some questions. One of those questions might be, 'What did Jesus come to rescue the world from? Why do we need to be rescued?'

To answer that question, we have to go all the way back to the beginning of all beginnings. The story is in the first book of the Bible, named Genesis. And the story continues through the whole Bible to the very last chapter.

From Adam* to Abraham*

The Bible begins with God. God has always been. And God decided to make the world. He made the heavens. He made the earth. And he filled them with good things. Then God made a man named Adam. He made a woman named Eve.* He put them in a beautiful garden. He gave them all that they needed. They could eat the fruit of every tree in the garden. And each time they ate, they could give thanks to the God who made them. But God told them that there was only one thing that they could not do. They could not eat from one of the trees in the middle of the garden. The fruit from that tree would not be good for them. If they ate from that tree, they would die. Each time they did not eat from the tree, they showed that they honored* the God who made them and gave them all good things.

One day, a snake came into the garden. Satan,* the Evil One,* used the snake to tell Eve a lie. He told her to eat the fruit that God told them not to eat. He told her that nothing bad would happen to them. So, they chose to believe* that lie. They chose not to obey God. They ate the fruit. When they did, they turned away from the God who made them. They did not honor God. They sinned.* Now they could not live with God in the place he had made for them. God sent them away from the garden. And they could never return there. They would have to live outside of the garden until they died. But God loved the man and woman that he had made. And he did not leave them. He watched over them. He gave them clothes to cover them. He gave them children. And he gave them a promise. God said that he would give them a son. He said that one day, that son would crush the head of the snake, the Evil One.

After Adam and Eve left the garden, many things happened. One of their sons killed his brother. Their children and their children's children grew more in number. They built cities. But, like

Adam and Eve, they did not honor God. They sinned. As more and more people began to live on the earth, they became more and more evil.*

So, God decided to send a flood to the earth. The flood would destroy all of the people and animals from the earth. But God made a plan to rescue some of the people and animals that he had made. God chose one man and his family to remain alive. His name was Noah.* Noah would build a large boat. He would bring some of the animals into the boat with him. After the flood, Noah and his family would start over again. They would fill the earth with children and teach them to follow God. And God did send the flood, just as he had promised. The waters from that flood covered the earth for many days.

After the flood, Noah and his family came out of the boat. They built houses. They had children. Soon the earth began to be filled with people again. But, still, not all of the people followed God. Instead, some of them built a tall building to honor themselves. God was not pleased. So, God confused the people. He changed the languages they spoke. They could not understand each other. So they moved away from each other. They moved to many places on the earth. They became different nations.

From Abraham to Moses*

Many years went by. But God was not finished with the people on the earth. He had a plan to rescue them, as he had rescued Noah and his family. So God chose a man named Abram.* God made him a promise. He told Abram that he would bless* him. He would give him a land of his own. He would give him a son. Then, God changed Abram's name to Abraham. God told Abraham that he would bless all of the nations because of him.

Later, Abraham did have a son. His name was Isaac.* Isaac became a man and also had a son. His name was Jacob.* Jacob grew to be a man and he had 12 sons. God changed Jacob's name too. He called him Israel.* And the sons of Jacob became known as the children of Israel.

After many years, there was a time when there was no food in the land that God gave to Abraham. So Jacob and his family moved to Egypt.* Not many years after they moved to Egypt, the king of Egypt made them slaves. They lived there for 400 years. But God did not leave the people he had chosen.

From Moses to David*

One day, God came to a man named Moses. God told Moses that he was going to take the children of Israel back to the land that God gave Abraham. This was a very difficult task. But God helped Moses. And, after all the children of Israel came out of Egypt, God made another promise. He told them that he would bless them. He would give them the land that he promised Abraham. And they would become a great nation.

God also gave Israel rules to help them live for God. When they obeyed God's ways, God would bless them. If they did not obey, God would not bless them. But if the people did not obey him, God made a way that they could be right with him again. The people could confess* to God and make a sacrifice* to God. Then, God would forgive* them for what they had done. The animal would die as a sacrifice so that the one who sinned could live.

After many years and after many troubles, the people did go into the land that God gave them. They lived there for many years. God was with them. He sent men and women to lead them. These leaders were called judges.*

From David to exile*

But the people of Israel wanted to be ruled like other nations. So, God gave the people what they wanted: a king. The first king did not follow God. So, God gave them a second king. His name was David.* Just like he had with Abraham and Moses, God made a special promise to David. He promised to make a great nation from his family. He promised that one of David's sons would rule Israel. This son would also be the king of all of the nations in all of the world. His kingdom* would last forever.

While David was king, God blessed Israel. David built a great kingdom. The people were strong. The land was safe. David was not a perfect man, but he loved God.

David had a son named Solomon.* After David died, Solomon

became king. God made him great too. Solomon built a special house for God called the temple.* The temple was a place where the people came to worship* God. But, after Solomon died, there was trouble in the land of Israel.

The people did not want Solomon's son to be the next king. So, Israel was no longer one nation. It broke apart. The people in the north part of the country chose a different king. They took the name Israel. The people in the south chose their own king. They took the name Judah.* Sometimes, Judah had a good king who told them to follow the ways of God. But Israel did not have kings who pleased God. And, for many years, the two nations fought with each other.

But God did not leave the people he had chosen. In those days, God spoke to his people through special men and women. These people were called prophets. They told the people to come back to God. They said that God would punish them if they did not return to him. God would let their enemies come and take them away from the land. Their enemies would take Israel and Judah from their land to a land that was not their own.

God warned them. But they did not listen. So, God sent an army to fight against Israel. They overcame Israel. They took the people from the land. Many years later, God sent another army. They fought against Judah. They destroyed the temple. They took the people from the land. It was a very sad time for God's people. But God sent prophets to comfort them. The prophets said that God loved them, and he would not forget them. He would remember the promises that he had made to them. And, one day, God would bring them back to the land that he promised to Abraham.

From exile to return

For many years, the people of God lived in exile. But, one day, God brought many of the people back to the land. The first thing they did was put the temple back together. Then, they built the walls of the city again. And soon, God sent leaders to remind them of the ways Moses had taught them to live. The people of Israel came back to their land.

But they were not a great nation any longer. They had no king. People still had to make sacrifices to be right with God. But the prophets told them to have hope.* God keeps his promises and would still keep the promises he made to Abraham, Moses and David. God would send the son he promised Abraham. God would live among his people like he had promised Moses. God would give a son from David's family who would rule all of the nations.

From return to Jesus

So, the people waited. For almost 400 years, there was no new word from God. No prophets spoke. No kings came to rule. But God did not leave the people he had chosen.

One day, an angel* came to a young virgin* named Mary.* He told her that God had chosen to do a miracle* in her. She would have a son. That son would have no man as a father. This son would be called the Son of God.* God said that this son would sit on the throne* of David. He was to be given the name, Jesus.

Soon, Mary did give birth to a son. They named him Jesus. God had become a man. And each day, Jesus grew tall and grew wise. When he grew to be an adult, he chose some men to be his followers.* They went from place to place with him. They heard him say and do many wonderful things. He made blind people see again. He made sick people well again. He even went to people who had died and gave them life again. They saw that he was a holy* man. He did nothing evil.* He always obeyed the laws* of Moses. He did not sin.*

Many people were happy to hear what Jesus said. But many of the people did not believe him. Some of the leaders became angry with him. They said that Jesus spoke in a way that made people think that Jesus was God. They were right. That made the leaders so angry that they decided to kill him.

So, Jesus met with his followers and told them what was going to happen. Soldiers were going to take Jesus and hold him. They were going to kill him. But his followers did not have to be afraid. God would bring Jesus back to life again. And that is just what happened.

But Jesus did not die only because men were angry with him. Jesus died to do something much more important. In Jesus, God was showing his love for the world. Jesus died to make a way that we could be right with God. On the cross,* God punished Jesus for sins he never committed. Jesus took the punishment that a world of sinful* people deserved. He suffered and died as a sacrifice to God. Now people would not have to make sacrifices anymore. Jesus took the punishment that all people would someday have to face. And to show that God accepted the sacrifice that Jesus made, God raised him from the dead.

After Jesus rose from the dead, he spent some time teaching the men and women who believed him. He told them that he would go to be with God soon. But, one day, he would return. When he returns, he will do all of the things that God had promised to Abraham, Moses, and David. But, until then, Jesus told all of his followers to go everywhere and tell everyone the good news about him. They were to say that Jesus is the Son of God. He died and is alive again. All people have sinned. And their sins have separated them from God. But anyone who believes in Jesus, anyone who trusts* his words, will have life that lasts forever. God will forgive them for the evil things that they have done. And, some day, they will live with God. They will go to a place where everything is good and they will never die. But, until then, they would not be alone. Jesus would send the Holy Spirit* to help them.

After Jesus finished saying these things, God took him up through the clouds. And so the followers did what Jesus told them to do. They went everywhere they could go. They told everyone they could tell about Jesus.

From Jesus to now

After many years, God came to one of the first men to follow Jesus named John.* He gave him a dream. He showed him many things about what will happen in the future. He told him that life will be hard for the Christians. He told him that Satan will fight against God and lie to many people. But he told John not to be afraid. Jesus will return to earth. He will defeat Satan. He will judge everyone that ever lived. He will punish Satan and all of those who followed him. And he will gather his people to be with him forever. He will make a new heaven* and a new earth. And he will rule all of the nations. They will be his people. He will be their God forever.

But that is not the end of the story. In some ways, a new story will just be beginning.

So, what do you think?

Now that you know the story, you must decide something. It is the same thing everyone who has ever heard the story must decide. Do you believe that the story is true? Will you decide to follow Jesus?

Most people can see that the world is not like God intended it to be. We live in a broken world and we are broken too. People make us sad and sometimes we are not happy with ourselves either. We do things that are not good. We think things are not good. Like Adam and Eve, we have not honored the God who made us.

But God loves us and he has been kind to us. He has made a way for us, and for our world to be right with God. But we must believe that Jesus is the son of God. We must believe that he died and is alive again. We must believe in Jesus and trust* his words and we will have life that lasts forever. God will forgive us for the evil things that we have done. And, some day, we will live with God. We will go to a place where everything is good. And we will never be sick or sad or hurt or cry or feel shame. But, until then, we will not be alone. Jesus has sent his Holy Spirit to help us to live a new life.

But following Jesus will not be easy. Satan, the Evil One,* does not want you to honor God. Many people did not like what Jesus said. Some people hated him so much that they wanted to take his life. When you follow Jesus, some people will not be pleased with you. They may even hate you as they hated Jesus. But if you follow Jesus, he will always be with you to guide you and help you.

So, what will you choose? You can choose to live the way you have always lived. You can believe the story that you have always believed. You can trust that your own way is the best way to live. Or you can believe that the story of Jesus is true. Jesus is the Son of God. He lived and died and rose again to rescue people just like you. The only way to be right with God is to trust Jesus. Believe in him. And follow him.

What can you do?

Do you see that the story of Jesus is true? Do you want to trust Jesus to rescue you? Do you want to follow him? Here is what you can do.

Talk to God

The first thing to do is talk to God. He listens. He has known you since you were first born. There has never been a word that you have spoken that he has not heard. So now, speak to him. Thank him for his great love for you. Tell God that you know that you have done many things that have not pleased him. You know that you need God to show you mercy.* But you have not and could not earn the mercy that you need. So, believe and accept that what he said is true. Trust Jesus to rescue you. Ask God to forgive you and welcome you as one of his people. You could use words like these when you talk to God:

> Dear God,
>
> I know that I have done many wrong things that have not pleased you. I do not deserve your mercy. I did not know you or follow you. I need to be forgiven.
>
> Thank you for loving me. Thank you for sending your son to die for people like me so that I could be forgiven. Thank you for bringing Jesus back to life. I ask you to give me a new life too.
>
> I now submit* to Jesus as my ruler and Lord.* Please help me to become the person that you made me to be.
>
> Amen.*

Follow Jesus

Submit to Jesus and begin to do what Jesus did. Start by talking to God as often as you can. That is what Jesus did. Ask God to be with you and guide you in his ways. Ask God to help you see the things in your life that need to change. You may have old habits that do not honor God. Perhaps you are angry or selfish or you hurt other people. Ask God to change those bad things and make new habits that would honor him. Ask God to make you kind and patient. Ask him to give you courage to follow him in every way.

If you do not have a Bible, ask God to help you find one. Read the scriptures.* As you read the scriptures, God will show you how to live. God will use those words to make you wise when you do not know what to do. And God will use those words to make you strong when you need help.

Do your best to find other people who follow Jesus. We call the people who gather together to worship Jesus, the church.* These are like your brothers and sisters in the family of God. Meet with them. Learn from them. Pray with them. We cannot follow Jesus well if we try to do it alone. God expects us to depend on one another and encourage one another as we follow Jesus.

Keep Trusting

Never forget that you have been put right with God because of what Jesus did for you. We all need to remember this. Because we will not be perfect even when we try hard and trust God. We will sometimes do things that will not please God. We may fail to love as we should or even fall back into an old, sinful habit. When we do, we must ask God to forgive us and change us. We must ask God to help us to love him with all of our hearts* and mind and strength. God begins his work to make us more and more like Jesus when we believe. His work will continue until we go to be with Jesus or when Jesus comes again to be with us.

Word
List

How it works

This Word List will help you better understand this book. Any word in the book with an * beside it is defined in this list. Sometimes, a word can have more than one meaning. This list will include the meanings that help you understand what you read.

A

Abraham/Abram

Abraham is the father of all of the Jews.* His name was Abram. Then God changed his name. God made a promise to him. He said that Abraham's family would become a great nation. God would bless* all of the other nations through one of his children.

Adam

Adam was the first man that God made. God made Adam from the dust of the ground.

Adopt/Adoption

Adoption is the legal act that brings a person into one's family. That person is now brought up as one's own child. Before, we were strangers to God and God's enemies. But now God has called us his own dear children.

Adultery

Adultery means to have sex with someone who is not your own wife or husband.

Altar

A table (usually stone) where the priest* burned the meat from animals and gave other gifts as a sacrifice* to God or false gods; a tall structure with a flat top where the priest puts the sacrifice to God or a false god; the 'holy* table.'

Amen

A word used to show that we agree. It means 'this is true' or 'may it be so.'

Ancestor

A person from your family who lived long ago.

Angel

An angel is a servant from God to bring his messages. An angel is a spirit.* An angel says good things about God. An angel does what God wants. An angel does good for people who are in Gods family. A bad angel is working for the Devil.*

Apostle

An Apostle was a man sent to speak for Jesus.* Jesus chose these men. Each of them spent time with Jesus. Each of them saw Jesus after he came back from death. God used them to start his church* and give us the New Testament.* A person sent to bring a message.

B

Babylon/ Babylonian

Babylon was a nation to the north of Israel.* For many years, it was an enemy of Judah.* One day, Babylon came into Judah and took many people away into exile.*

Baptism/Baptize

A church* leader puts a person under water for a moment. Then the person is brought up out of the water. In this way we show that Christ has made us clean. We also show to everyone that we are part of the church.* When we are baptized it reminds us of Jesus who died. Men placed him in a grave. But he rose from death.

Believer

A believer is a person who knows and trusts Christ.

Bible

Another name for the scripture;* the writings of the prophets* and the apostles;* all of the books of the Old and New Testaments.*

Bless

To say or do something good for someone; to speak well of someone; to give things to someone to honor them; to ask God to do good to someone; to call for good things to happen to someone; to set someone apart for a special benefit.

Blessed

A word to call someone who receives many good things; a word to call someone who is kept holy.*

Blessings

Blessings are the good things that God does for us. When we ask God to bless us, we ask him to help us and do good in us.

C

Christ

Christ is a title that is used to name Jesus.* It means 'the chosen one.' It is a way that the early Christians* said that Jesus was the Messiah,* the One God had chosen.

Christian

The word Christian means one who follows Christ.* This was not a name that Christians chose for themselves. People started calling them Christians because they were always talking about Christ. They followed what Jesus* taught. They lived the way Jesus lived.

Church

The church is a group of people that follow and believe all about Jesus Christ. They meet together. They baptize* believers.* They eat the Lord's Supper. They obey the teaching of Christ.

Community

A community is a group of people who share something in common. They may live in or near the same place. Or they could share a common belief. The church is a community of people who share a common belief in Jesus.

Conceive

The moment of making a baby when a new life begins in a woman's body.

Confess/Confession

To say that you have done wrong things; to say that you believe* in God.

Content

To be content is to be happy with what we have. To know that what we have is enough.

Corinth

Corinth was a city in Asia. Many people travelled through that city. Paul* helped to take the good news there. He sent letters to Corinth to help the church* there.

Covenant

When two or more people agree together; when God and people agree to something by making a promise; when God and a person or people agree to a special thing.

Creation/Created

When God made the world and everything there is; everything that God has made; what God did when he made everything from nothing.

Creator/ Maker

Creator is the name used for God because he made all things. He created* all of the things that we can see and things we cannot see.

Cross

A cross is two pieces of wood fixed together. When Jesus lived, people fixed criminals to a cross in order to kill them. Jesus died on a cross.

Curse

A powerful word that can bring harm or punishment on someone or something.

D

David

David was the king of all of Israel.* God made a promise to David. He told David that one of his sons would be king forever.

Devil

Devil is another name for Satan.* Satan* is the worst of the bad angels*: *See angel.*

Disciple

A disciple is a person who follows another person and learns from him. A person who believes in Jesus. A person who follows what Jesus teaches.

Doxology

A doxology is a song or words of praise that people use to honor God. Sometimes a doxology is sung or spoken at the end of a prayer or worship.

E

Egypt

Egypt was a land to the south of Israel.* The sons of Jacob* lived in Egypt* for many years until Moses* came to lead them out. When Jesus* was a small boy, his family went there for a while.

Elijah

Elijah was a prophet.* He spoke for God to the people of Israel.* The king did not like Elijah. The queen did not like him either. But God watched over him. He did many wonders in Israel. He overcame many of the prophets who served false gods.

Elisha

Elisha was a prophet.* For many years, he helped Elijah.* When Elijah went to be with God, Elisha took his place. He did many wonders in the land. God gave him great power.

Eternal

Things that have always been or will always continue to be are eternal. A thing that has no beginning or ending.

Eve

Eve was the first woman God made. God made Eve from a bone from Adam's side.

Everlasting

Things that continue forever.

Evil

Bad; the opposite of good; wicked; doing bad; things that hurt someone.

Evil One

Another name for Satan.* He is the one who works against God and God's people. The Evil One is sometimes called the Devil.

Exile/Exiles

People who have to leave their own land, often for a long time; the times when the Jews* were taken from the land of Israel.*

Ezekiel

Ezekiel was a priest* and a prophet.* He lived in Babylon* during the exile.* He spoke for God to the people there. God asked him to do many strange things to get his message to the people. He always obeyed. He told them that God would punish Babylon. And they would go back to their home land someday.

F

Faith

Faith means to believe in someone or something. To trust* and believe in God. To know that God is real, even when we cannot see him.

Faithful/ Faithfulness

To be full of faith* and not moving from what you think is true; to do the right thing; to follow God's ways.

Follower

A person who goes along with someone who leads; the men and women who believe* in Jesus* and do what he says.

Forgive/ Forgiven

To forgive is to show love and not to remember bad things against someone. When God forgives us, he does not hold the wrong things we do against us.

G

Galatia

Galatia was an area north of Israel.* There were many towns and villages there. Many people from that area heard the good news about Jesus.* Paul* wrote a letter to help the church* there.

Gentiles

Gentile was the name given to any people that were not Jews.* No matter what nation people came from, if they were not Jews, they were called Gentiles. People who did not know the God of the Jews.

Glory

God's glory is everything that makes God beautiful and great, like a great king.

Gospel

The good news for everybody that God saves people from sin* through Jesus* Christ;* the good news of the things Jesus has done for us by his life, death and rising from the dead; the message from God to us; the four books at the beginning of the New Testament.*

Grace

Grace is a gift of God that we do not deserve because of the bad things we have done. Grace is what God gives because he is so kind to us. The forgiveness* and help that comes from God.

Guilt/Guilty

When we know we have done wrong things and feel bad about them; when we feel shame for wrong things we have done.

Hagar

Hagar was Sarah's maid. Abraham* had a child with her. This caused many problems.

Heart

The heart is the most important part of a person. The part of a person that feels and thinks and decides things.

Heaven

Heaven is the place where God and Christ are. God lives and rules there. Heaven is the place where people who know God and Jesus will go after they die. The place where people will always be happy and have no troubles. The new heaven and the new earth is the future home of the people who know God.

Hebrew/ Hebrews

The language of the Jews;* another name for a Jew; a person from Israel.* The letter in the New Testament that is written by Paul for the Jews.

Hell

Hell is a place where God has separated wicked people from himself. Hell is the place of punishment for wicked people after death.

Holy

To be holy is to be set apart for God. To be like God is to be godly. When we are holy, we are without sin. We are clean before God.

Holy Spirit

God's Spirit. The Spirit whom Jesus sent to help people. The Holy Spirit is another name for God. Also called the Spirit of God, the Spirit of Christ and the Spirit that helps us. The Holy Spirit is a person but is not human as we are. He is God, equal with God the Father and with God the Son: *See also Trinity.* He does the work of God among the people in the world. Nobody sees the Holy Spirit but he lives with and in those that know Jesus.

Honor

To honor someone is to speak well of a person. To act well toward a person because you respect and value them.

Honorable

To act well. To live in a way that shows respect for God and for people. To be a person who does good and right things.

Hope

To look for a future thing that God has promised.

Idol

An idol is a thing made of wood, stone or metal which people worship* instead of worshipping God. An idol is a picture of a person or a thing one loves instead of God. An idol is a false god. Something that somebody loves more than God.

Idolatry

Idolatry is the practice of worshipping idols. The worship of false gods. When someone loves something more than they love God.

Isaac

Isaac was the son of Abraham.* God gave him to Abraham in his old age. He was the son that God had promised him.

Isaiah

Isaiah was a prophet* in Judah.* He spoke for God to the kings of Judah. He wrote a book that is part of the Major Prophets.*

Israel

The land where the Jewish people lived. The people of Israel is another name for the Jewish people. They are the children of Abraham, Isaac, and Jacob.

J

Jacob

Jacob was the son of Isaac.* He had many sons. God spoke with Jacob and changed his name to Israel.* His children became known as the children of Israel. When there was no food in the land, they went to Egypt* to find food. Jacob died there. His family stayed there for 400 years.

James

James was a leader in the first church.* He was a brother of Jesus.* He wrote a letter that is part of the Bible.

Jeremiah

Jeremiah was a prophet* to the people who lived in Jerusalem.* He lived before the city was burned.

Jerusalem

Jerusalem was the city where David* lived. Solomon* built the temple* there. It was the most important city of Judah.*

Jesus

Jesus is the Son of God.* He came into the world to rescue people from their sin.* He is the Messiah* that the people of God had waited for.

Jew/Jewish

A Jew is a person that is born from Abraham, Isaac and Jacob, and their children. A person that has the faith* of the Jews.

John

John was an Apostle.* He was a very close friend of Jesus* as well. He listened carefully to Jesus and wrote many of the things he said in his book. When he was an old man, God gave him a vision.* He wrote what he saw in the last book of the Bible.*

John the Baptist

John the Baptist was the man who went before Jesus* to prepare the way. He called people to turn from their sin.* He baptized* Jesus.

Jonah

Jonah was a prophet.* God told him to go speak to Nineveh.* Jonah tried to run away. A big fish swallowed him. Then he did what God asked him to do. But he was not happy when people turned back to God.

Joseph

Joseph was the favorite son of his father Jacob.* His brothers hated him. They sold him to people who were going to Egypt.* He faced many difficult things. But God used him to rescue his family when there was no food to eat.

Joshua

When Moses* died, Joshua became the leader of God's people. He led them into the land God promised them.

Judah

Judah was one of the sons of Jacob.* When his father was dying, he blessed* him. He said that his family would rule the others. David* was from that family. Many years later, Jesus* was born from the family of Judah. Judah was also the name the people gave to the southern part of Israel.* After the nation divided, the land in the north was called Israel. The land in the south was called Judah.

Judas

Judas was one of the disciples of Jesus. He was also known as Judas Iscariot. He was the one who turned Jesus over to his enemies. He betrayed Jesus with a kiss.

Judges

God chose new leaders for Israel* after Joshua died. These men and women were called judges. They helped to deliver Israel from its enemies.

Judgement

When God says what is right or wrong; when someone says who is good or bad; when people are tested or judged by God; the day when Christ* will judge all people is called the day of judgement.

Just/Justice

The quality of being completely fair and being right; the way that God is right in dealing with all that he has made; the correct thing that God does with all that he has made.

K

Kingdom

A kingdom is where a king rules. A land where a king rules. The kingdom of God is where God rules.

L

Lamb

A small sheep like the animals given as a sacrifice* to God in the temple.* A baby sheep.

Law

Rules that a ruler makes to tell people how to live. The rules God gave Moses for the people of Israel.

Lord

Lord is the name for God in the Bible. It means that he is above all other things and ruler of all things. A name that we use for Jesus when we obey him.

Luke

Luke was a man who followed Jesus.* He was not an Apostle.* But he knew many of these men and heard their stories. He sometimes went with Paul* on his trips. His book about Jesus is in the Bible.* It is one of the gospels.*

M

Mark

Mark was a young man when he began to follow Jesus.* He spent time with Peter.* He told the story of Jesus in the book that bears his name.

Mary

Mary was the mother of Jesus.* She cared for him as a boy. She was there when he died on the cross.* Remember: There are many different women named Mary in the New Testament.*

Mary Magdalene

Mary Magdalene was a woman who followed Jesus. When she met Jesus, she had evil spirits living in her. Jesus made the spirits leave.

Matthew

Matthew collected taxes before he met Jesus.* Jesus called him to leave his job and follow him. Matthew was an Apostle.*

Mediator

A mediator is someone who speaks for the interests of one person to another person. A mediator helps settle problems between people and brings people together.

Mercy/Merciful

Being kind to bad people; help to those who are in need or difficulty; the love God shows in forgiving;* God's love and goodness; God's pity towards all he has made.

Messiah

Messiah is a title for the special servant of God. It means 'the one God chose to anoint.'* Samuel* put oil on David* to show that God had chosen him to be king. So the Jews* used the name Messiah to refer to the king that God promised to send from David's family. This king would rescue the people from all of their enemies. He was the king who would build God's kingdom.* That kingdom would last forever. When Jesus* came, he said that he was the Messiah that the Jews had waited for. He was the Christ.* Christ is the Greek word for Messiah. But many of the Jews did not believe* him.

Miracle

Wonderful works that God does by his power; a wonderful thing that shows that a person's message is from God.

Moses

Moses was born in Egypt* when Jacob's* family lived there. God chose Moses to help the Jews.* He rescued them and brought them out of Egypt.

Muslim

People who believe in one god whom they call Allah. They teach that a man named Muhammed was the greatest of all prophets. Their holy book is called the Koran.

N

Neighbor

A neighbor is someone who lives close to another person. The Jews* did not think anyone who was not also a Jew was their neighbor. But Jesus said we are to think of everyone as our neighbor.

New Testament

The last part of the Bible,* which the writers wrote after Jesus* rose up from the dead. It is about the things that Jesus did and taught. It is also about the church.*

Noah

Noah was the man God chose to build a boat. When the flood came, Noah and his family were safe in the boat. God covered the land with water and all of the other people died. God told Noah and his family to fill the earth with people again.

Offering

A gift for God (or false gods) from the priest* and people; an animal to be offered as a sacrifice.*

Old Testament

The first part of the Bible;* the holy* books that men wrote before Jesus* was born.

Parable

A story, like those told by Jesus,* to explain the things that he taught; a saying or a story from which you can understand more than one thing; a story where part of the meaning is hidden.

Passover

An important holy* day for the Jews.* They ate a special meal on this day every year. This was to remember that God freed them from being slaves in Egypt* at the time of Moses.*

Paul/Saul

Paul was a man who did not believe* in Jesus.* His name was Saul then. Jesus came to him and made him an Apostle.* That is when Jesus changed his name to Paul. He wrote many letters. Some of those letters are now in the Bible.*

Peace

When we do not fight God or other people; when we have no troubles in our mind or spirit;* when we are friendly to other people.

Peter/Simon Peter

Peter was an Apostle.* He was one of the first people to see Jesus* after he came back from death. God used him to help the church* get started.

Philip

Philip served the new church* in Jerusalem.* He helped give food to the widows there. God used him to tell many people about Jesus in many places.

Philippi

Philippi was a city in Asia. Paul* went there to tell people the good news about Jesus.* Many people there believed.*

Philippians

Philippians were people from the city of Philippi.* There were many people there who believed* the good news about Jesus.* Paul wrote a letter to the church* there. He wanted to thank them for helping him do his work. That letter is now part of the Bible.*

Praise

To say how good a person is; to tell God how great he is, as when we are praying and singing to him.

Priests

The priests in Israel* were the men who helped people worship* God. The priests began to do this work when Moses* was the leader. They took care of God's Tent. They made sacrifices* for the people. When Solomon* built the temple,* they took care of it. They served the people up until the time that Jesus* lived and for many years after. There were also priests in other nations. They sacrificed to false gods.

Prophet

A prophet was one who was able to tell other people what God wanted. Prophets spoke for God a long time ago. Someone who told things that would happen in the future.

Prosper

To prosper is to enjoy good things. To prosper is to be in good health or be rich. We prosper when people speak well of us. We prosper when we enjoy the kindness of other people.

Psalms/Psalm

Songs that tell God how good and great he is, and what he has done for us; songs for when we are praising God; one of the books of the Old Testament.*

R

Redeem/ Redeemed

To buy something back after it has been lost or taken. To pay a price to make something your own; what Christ* did when he gave his life so that God could forgive* us for the bad things we have done.

Repent

To repent is to turn from sin.* To do what God wants us to do. To decide not to do the bad things you did in the past.

Respect

Respect means to treat someone as if they are very valuable.

Resurrection

Resurrection means to be raised from death. To come alive again.

Reveal/ Revelation

To reveal something is to make it known. Something God makes known to people; Revelation is the name of the last book of the Bible.*

Righteous

To be righteous means to be right with God. The righteous are the people who are right with God. When God makes a person right with him, he sees that person as clean. A righteous person is God's friend and not his enemy.

Romans

Romans were the people who lived in the city of Rome.* Or they were people who lived in other places but were part of the nation that ruled from Rome.

S

Sabbath

The Sabbath was the day when God rested from His work of creation. The Sabbath was a day when God told the Jews* not to work. It was a special day when they rested and worshipped God.

Sacred

That which is set apart for God; something God has kept for himself; a thing that God makes holy.*

Sacrifice

To kill an animal as an offering* to God so that God will forgive* an evil* thing. The Israelites* were told to make sacrifices to God. Usually, it was a special animal that the priests* killed and burned on the altar.* Some people made sacrifices to false gods. Something a person gives up for a special purpose can also be called a sacrifice; giving up something that is important to you on behalf of someone (God); offering yourself to work for God; Christ's* death for us.

Samaria

Samaria was a city in Israel.* It was the capital of the northern kingdom.* Samaria was also the name given to the territory around that city.

Samson

Samson was a judge* in Israel.* He had long hair. That hair was a sign that he was set apart for God. God made him very strong. He won many battles. But he was not careful to obey God. He killed many of the enemies of God when he died.

Samuel

Samuel was the last of the judges* of Israel.* He was also a prophet.* God used him to make David* the king of Israel.*

Sarah

Sarah was the wife of Abraham.* God changed her name from Sarai to Sarah. God promised that she would have a son when she was old. She gave birth to a son named Isaac.*

Save/Salvation

Salvation is when God rescues us from the results and power of sin.* To be saved or rescued from bad things.

Satan

Satan is another name for Devil.* Satan* is the worst of the bad angels*: See angel.

Savior

Jesus Christ is the Savior. Someone who brings us back to God and rescues us from being punished for the bad things we have done.

Scripture

The writings of God's holy* words; another name for the Bible;* the book which tells God's truth and shows that Jesus is Lord,* the Savior* and Messiah.*

Shepherd

A person who cares for a group of sheep. The Bible* sometimes says that God is like a shepherd. He cares for his people. Jesus* said that he was the good shepherd. He would give his life for his people (sheep).

Sin/ Sinful/Sinned

Sin is the wrong things that people do against God or against other people. When we do not follow the rules that God made, we sin. When we do not do what God wants us to do, we sin. All people are sinful because they do things against God or other people. All people are sinful because they were born with bad desires.

Sinner

A person who breaks God's rules; a person who does things against God.

Solomon

Solomon was David's* son. He was the king after David died. God made him very wise.

Son of God

Son of God is a title. It is used to speak of Jesus* in the New Testament.* It means that Jesus comes from God the Father. Christians* can also become the sons of God. This happens when they believe* in Jesus and he makes them a part of God's family.

Soul

The soul is the part of a person that we cannot see that is in us during our life, and lives after we die. God gave a soul to Adam and Eve when he breathed life into them. The soul of a person is sometimes called the person's spirit*: See spirit.

Spirit

A spirit is a being that does not have a body, and no one can see it. God is spirit. God made other spirit beings (angels*) that we cannot see, who can be good or bad. The soul* of a person is sometimes called the person's spirit: See soul.

Submit

To put yourself under the authority or care of someone else. If you submit to someone's authority, you accept that they have power over you.

Synagogue

A place where the Jews met to worship God and study the scriptures.

T

Temple

The Temple was the place that Solomon* built for God. Israel* went there to worship* God. The priests* made sacrifices* there. It was the place where God would come and live with his people. The temple was in the city of Jerusalem.* Other nations built temples. They went to those places to honor false gods.

Tempt/Temptation

To test someone or to try to make them do bad things. A temptation is something that causes someone to want to do evil.

Testament

Another word for covenant;* a special agreement or promise. When God and people agree to a special thing, they make a covenant.* An agreement between two or more people.

Throne

A special chair where a king sits. It is the place the king rules from.

Tomb

A tomb is a place where people put a dead body. A place where people bury a body.

Tribe

A group that has a common beginning or purpose. The sons of Jacob* each had families. Those families became known as the tribes of Israel.* The tribes were named after the sons of Jacob.

Trinity

Trinity is the word we use to speak of the One God that is three persons: God the Father, God the Son (Jesus), and God the Holy Spirit.*

Trust

To trust is to follow something or somebody you think is true. To have faith* and act with faith*: See faith.

Virgin

A virgin is a person who has not had sex.

Vision

A dream that someone can have while they are awake. In the Bible,* God uses visions to speak to his people. God gave the prophets* visions to show what he wanted them to say to the people. Not all visions come from God.

Womb

The part of the woman's body where she carries a baby until it is born.

Worship

To worship is to show God that he is great and that we love him very much. To worship is to give honor* and thanks to God: See honor. What we should do when we are with God.

Wrath

What a person feels when they are very angry; what a person does when they are very angry. The wrath of God is the right thing he feels when he is angry with sin;* the right thing God does when he is angry with people who sin.

Topic
Index

Scripture Index

The Old Testament

The New Testament

Dedication

I write this book with a hope that it will honor God and bring honor to the people who have helped me write it.

My grandfather, Leland Webber, loved the Bible. His passion for it helped me love it too. Professor Fred Zaspel, a true scholar and long-time friend, made many suggestions that helped guide my work. I cannot think of a place where I did not find his advice helpful.

A special thank you to Leah Seier of Editorial Service by Leah. Her expertise and care were deeply appreciated as we worked through the multiple rewrites of this book. Thank you to my friend Susan Moore whose eye for consistency and clarity, both in language and theology, was a great help. This book is better because of her insights. Thank you also to Sandra Day, an ESL teacher whose accountant's eye seemed to catch every weak spot in the manuscript. Thank you to Jason Chittum of EC Design and Print (ecdesignandprint.com). Jason did both the layout and cover design for Simple Answers to Not So Simple Questions.

Special thanks to Itunu Mary Adepegba, who did the indexing for the book. Her work has made the book a much better tool to help our readers understand the scriptures.

Tom Castor
January 2021

About the Author

Tom Castor is the founder of the Clear and Simple Media Group, a ministry of the Baptist General Conference of Canada and Converge. Tom is a seasoned writer and communicator who has done pioneer mission work in the subarctic of Canada, church planting in a restricted access country in SE Asia, and story development work in Africa. He did his undergraduate work in Biblical studies and English literature, and he has a graduate degree in linguistics.

Clear and Simple Media produces content that is linguistically simple, theologically clear, and biblically faithful.